TANDEM

A DEVOTIONAL FOR *ADOPTING* WITH *GOD* IN THE LEAD

ALISON ENGLAND

ISBN 978-0-9982137-0-5

Tandem: A Devotional for Adopting with God in the Lead
Published by Winged Word Press
Buckeye, AZ 85396
www.wingedwordpress.com

Cover photo by Kelsey England
Cover design by Rachmad Agus Ridwan
Author photo by Indie Image Photo
Book layout by https://www.ebooklaunch.com

Names and identifying details in some personal stories herein have been altered in order to preserve the privacy of the individuals involved.

This book is dedicated to our Lord
and to those families that will forever be changed by His word
and through the blessing of adoption.

Contents

INTRODUCTION

When my husband and I sat down for our first consultation with our adoption attorney, Mark McDermott, his words were the nugget of hope we had been seeking. He put it simply, "If you want to adopt, you WILL adopt." These words encapsulated the commitment and determination that propelled us forward until the day we held our child in our arms.

The previous meetings we had with adoption agencies left us engulfed in doubt. Mark was the first person to dismantle our fundamental worry that adoption was uncertain. In a straightforward manner, he presented the facts and a sensible approach toward adoption. In two hours, he provided us with the outline of steps to take and a plan to get started. Mark captured the reality of adoption, which is this: it is an informed choice that is absolutely attainable with perseverance. My experience was that many people who initially 'counseled' us regarding adoption portrayed it as an evaluative process. The last thing I needed was someone telling me I was 'unworthy' of being a parent. In all reality, the only formal evaluative piece in the adoption process is the home study, which, unless you pick a fight with your social worker or have a criminal history, you are bound to pass.

Mark's final statement in our initial meeting was, "Adoption is certain, you just have to hang in there long enough." Here it is, the premise of a successful adoption, "How do you navigate the tough spots of adoption, so that you can withstand the journey?" If you can answer that question, your adoption was just stamped "Guaranteed."

I don't know how you arrived here, reading this book on adoption. But I have been in your place: thirsting for stories of hope, seeking a sliver of security. My purpose in writing this book is to provide you with a Godly resource that uplifts you and carries you through to the finish line. This is more than our sweet story of adopting our daughter, Annika. When doubt and stress flare up, I want you to be armed with the Lord's word and some practical guidance to overcome each trouble spot and jump to the next step.

Sharing our adoption story is emotional. Still several years post-finalization I cry when I tell others about Annika and our quest for her. To no surprise, those who walked alongside us on this journey feel the depths of emotion when we share about her adoption. But our story also touches acquaintances and strangers in a way that I did not expect. When I recount how Annika came to be part of our family, they are blindsided with teary eyes. I have witnessed enough salty drops to fill a bucket of pure awe, as they hear how God was planning for this child even before her creation. To think that He loves her *so* much that He would weave together such an intricate plan to nurture and care for this child is mighty powerful.

It is not just your child for whom the Lord has been planning; He has an amazing path mapped for you also. It is incredible to think that our Lord loves us *so* much that He was working in our lives even before your creation. God has expertly crafted your life experience to ensure that you are uniquely qualified to successfully endure the challenging adventure of adoption.

How one arrives at a decision to adopt varies tremendously. I have good friends that have gone through many years of self-sacrifice and frustration with unsuccessful infertility treatments.

Infertility is nothing less than devastating. This is not a new issue, yet infertility is one that is lined with such grief and desperation that thousands of years later we are still telling the stories of biblical women like Hannah and Elizabeth.

Many weathered couples find that at a certain point the cons of infertility treatment just out-weight the pros, and there is a shift in focus towards adoption. After countless shots, thousands of dollars, and calculated sex, some may start to wonder if there could be another plan in mind for them. I would venture to say that over half of the families in our adoption support group chose adoption instead of continuing with infertility treatments.

I have another friend who adopted after carrying two babies to term and losing both. The grief she experienced was more than one can imagine. Adoption became their means of having a family, and now they have a family of four.

Like us, others may have felt a nudge, a relentless tugging in their heart to adopt. Maybe it is recognized as God's voice calling, or maybe just an instinctive understanding of what needs to be done. I would encourage you to act on this innermost voice. Many women I have spoken to about our adoption share that they regret not acting on that voice they heard ten or twenty years ago.

Regardless of the reason for stepping out on this high-dive of adoption, once we jump in, we are all on the journey together. While our story is revealed through the lens of independent adoption, many of the same steps and trials exist with agency adoption, domestic, international and also foster adoption.

If you like Tandem and want to gain more encouragement for the journey, visit my blog at www.TandemAdoption.com or say hello on Instagram @ridingTandem. I would also like to invite you to be part of my closed Facebook group, Tandem: Adopting with God in the Lead. Chat directly with me and others along the adoption path. Request membership in this group today!

Adoption is a precious undertaking that will bring you closer to your Creator, open your eyes to His incredible ways, and ultimately bring a child into your arms. If you are reading this book right now, be encouraged…the Lord is working in your life!

1

AN OLD COUNTRY ROAD

The Beginning

A flat, desolate, horizon-to-horizon, cow-roaming southern Idaho expanse separated our home from the local elementary school where my daughter attended kindergarten. Each weekday, I made the round trip, driving her to and from class on a rough, rut-ridden road. It was an unenviable routine that came with my husband's Air Force assignment at Mountain Home Air Force Base. Each day the view was the same—sagebrush, an occasional rock and wind-blown tumbleweed mixed with swirling sand. As I drove this 20-mile stretch of desolation each day, I passed the only traffic control, which was a yellow sign that warned, "Watch for Stock," which was clearly not a personal finance reference.

To break up the monotony, Kelsey (our five-year-old daughter) and Alex (our two-year-old son) engaged with great intensity in the made-up "tumbleweed game." It was a simple challenge: tally the number of tumbleweeds we hit on the way to school. The tumbleweed game added to our plethora of homemade fun in Mountain Home, Idaho. With few organized sports and no YMCA, I charged myself with whipping up whimsical parties and forming a toddler-time music enrichment group. A city fish very much out of water, I grew lungs that allowed us to thrive in this rural culture.

I grew up in Newport Beach, California, where dirt was a little-known concept. Every plot of land had long since been turned into luxurious, landscaped vistas.

You might wonder how a California girl ended up in rural Idaho. Eleven years earlier, I said *I do* to the love of my life and, at the same time, silently said *I will* to the Air Force. I spent the first 18 years of my life nestled in the same beachside home and another four studying on the Malibu campus of Pepperdine University. Then, just one year after graduating from college, I married Joel and became an Air Force spouse. The six assignments leading up to our move to Idaho afforded us opportunities to become locals, *Kamaaina,* on an island paradise in Hawaii as well as live at the base of the majestic Rocky Mountains in Colorado Springs. This assignment was less luxurious than those had been, but I learned to appreciate the simplicity of my new life. This daily drive on the country road became bearable and, finally, enjoyable, as I learned to appreciate fewer stimuli and more openness.

Kelsey's kindergarten class was a gem, hidden away on the dusty Mountain Home Air Force Base. Surrounded by a fine teacher and kind children, Kelsey blossomed. She made friends with many other students, but one particular classmate named Ava stood out from the crowd. One day, I visited the kindergarten classroom and saw thirty or so bouncing little people settling into their chairs. The teacher was giving directions, to which a few of the kids were actually paying attention, but most (Kelsey included) preferred talking to their neighbors. It did not take long for me to see that Kelsey had a special friend who had blond hair, a soft round face, an inviting smile and bright blue eyes.

I could not resist the temptation. I leaned over to Kelsey and whispered, "Who is your friend with the blond hair?" Kelsey turned and said, "This is Ava. We play together." The teacher raised an eyebrow at my interference, and I quickly withdrew and sat back in my miniature chair. As I observed Kelsey's new friend, she stood out among the children as extraordinarily tenderhearted toward those around her who often scraped their knees or had their feelings hurt. That afternoon on the ride home, Kelsey begged for a playdate with Ava.

As any good Air Force spouse would, I started an inquiry the next day to find out who Ava's parents were so that I could invite her over to play with Kelsey. Quiet whispers shared that she lived with a foster family. The complexities of my playdate plan grew exponentially with that news. Over the course of the next few weeks, my many attempts to contact her foster parents were unsuccessful.

A few months into the school year, Ava arrived to class with a broken arm. Since I had become a classroom volunteer, I overheard a social worker telling the teacher that she would no longer live in that foster home. Her change of placement suggested that Ava had been the victim of child abuse, and I choked back my tears. Ava stood in the shadow of the cinder block hallway, and while she was naive to the uncertainty of her future, I knew the tragedy that lay before her—the certain loss and disappointment she would endure in the foster care system. I wanted to intervene, but as an experienced social worker, I knew that becoming licensed and eligible to foster Ava as a temporary Air Force family was not a possibility. The sadness tugged at my heart as I started my drive home from kindergarten that afternoon. The lack of resolution felt thick. I felt helpless. I stood by while a little girl was subjected to the against-the-odds luck of finding secure attachment with a loving family.

On the trip home, I watched Kelsey in the rear view mirror as she fell asleep. My next stop was to pick up Alex from a babysitter. The landscape I knew so well had blurred into an indistinct, monochromatic image without horizon or form. The hum of the engine dimmed, and my hands felt numb on the steering wheel as the car proceeded as if it were driving itself. My mind was lost in sadness for Ava.

It happened suddenly, not as a flash of lighting or an old man speaking from the back seat, but God's voice was loud and clear. His words penetrated me with the precision of a surgeon's laser. "You will adopt one of mine." I was jolted into clarity of purpose. Startled, but not in fear, I answered the voice, "Okay." I heard myself saying this out loud several times—first a hushed "Okay," and then with a more resolute commitment: "Okay!" I instantly understood the implication of my agreement. Tears flowed as the horizon and sky with its silvery clouds rode alongside me in the afternoon wind. My memory raced back to the few other times in my life when I had heard the Lord speaking to me. But this was the first time God's voice had been a directive. The words continued to resonate in my mind: "You will adopt one of mine."

I hastily picked up Alex, parked the car in the driveway and ushered Kelsey and Alex to their rooms where they played without my interference. I puttered around the house, looking at my watch and waiting for my husband to come home for lunch. I couldn't wait to tell him the great news that we were going to adopt a child. I must confess that, during the minutes (which seemed like hours) prior to my husband's arrival, I trembled with overwhelming emotion, using Kleenex to dry my tears. When he came through the door, I bolted to him and, in a frenzy of chaotic words, tried to explain what had happened. The words tumbled over each other in an avalanche of disjointed descriptions. Of course, it made little sense to my down-to-earth lawyer husband whose life was made up of meticulously organized thoughts. After patiently listening, he raised his hands to slow my wave of emotion and told me to slow down and logically explain what happened. I was on the witness stand, and he methodically asked clarifying questions.

He spoke softly, calmly and deliberately—his hallmark skill as a successful trial lawyer. It was not a surprise when Joel's reaction was a cautious approach. He said, "Well, let's pray about this and revisit it later," and gave me a comforting hug that shouted, "I love you, even when you have crazy ideas!" I realized that I would have to take a deep breath and present my case at a time more favorable to his acceptance of a rather life-altering scenario.

The Lord called me that fall afternoon to adopt, but He had been preparing Joel and me all along. In fact, as I look back, it is nearly impossible to find the exact starting point of the Lord's preparation of us for this journey.

Ava's plight softened my heart so that I heard God's voice. It was a life-impacting moment on that old country road where our life story took a hard turn. Many of the adoptive parents I have become friends with in the past few years share stories of their life-impact moment-the loss of a child or the doctor's appointment at which the nasty word "infertility" was muttered. If you are arriving at the idea of adoption due to loss or struggle, I am not suggesting that God is at the root of this loss. Your suffering is one of the deepest and most difficult to navigate. You may find yourself restless, tired, fractured, scared, lonely and loaded with worry. Yet the Lord says, "...our suffering gives us the strength to go on. The strength to go on produces character. Character produces hope." (Romans 5:3-4)

As you stand on the precipice of adoption, your launching off point is not merely a platform of suffering, it is a high-dive of hope. Like many, I am uncertain why bad things happen to good people. What I do know is this: He has a plan for you. "For I know the plans I have for you," declares the LORD, "plans to prosper you and not to harm you, plans to give you hope and a future." (Jeremiah 29:11)

We look ahead with hope, but we also need to reflect on how we arrived here. In Rick Warren's book *The Purpose Driven Life*, he encourages his readers to "Examine your experiences and extract the lessons you have learned. Review your life and think about how it has shaped you."[1] Ephesians 5:17 states, "Don't act thoughtlessly, but understand what the Lord wants you to do." When you look back at your life, the experiences you've had, the people who have made an impact on you, do you see the arrows that have pointed you toward adoption? Those indicators are no accident!

We launch from the high-dive of adoption for different reasons. As you proceed on this adventure wrought with potholes, unforeseen curves and unexpected beauty, paste this scripture onto a billboard in your heart: "The LORD himself goes before you and will be with you; he will never leave you nor forsake you. Do not be afraid; do not be discouraged." (Deuteronomy 31:8)

He will unlock the doors that will lead you to your child. Be humbled, for the Lord has handpicked *you* to adopt one of His.

Scripture

Romans 5:3-4 (NIRV)
Our suffering gives us the strength to go on. The strength to go on produces character. Character produces hope.

Jeremiah 29:11
"For I know the plans I have for you," declares the LORD, "plans to prosper you and not to harm you, plans to give you hope and a future."

Ephesians 5:17 (NLV)
Don't act thoughtlessly, but understand what the Lord wants you to do.

Deuteronomy 31:8
The LORD himself goes before you and will be with you; he will never leave you nor forsake you. Do not be afraid; do not be discouraged.

Thoughts Along the Way

What is your beginning? What has brought you to this high-dive of adoption?

What is an example of your strength through your struggle? How has that impacted your character?

2

UNITED

Readiness

When I was a young girl, Knott's Berry Farm was not far from my Newport Beach home. It was the ultimate fun with its rustic, down-home-themed amusement park complete with country-fried chicken, Knott's boysenberry jam, enormous pickles in wooden barrels and dirt streets bordered by plank sidewalks.

So it was completely out of character when the park added a modern, spiral-formed, tubular metal roller coaster known as the Corkscrew. It was famous for its ability to propel riders through a series of gut-wrenching twirls and twists guaranteed to elicit screams from the most steadfast girls. The steel monster pummeled riders upside down over a reflection pond, thereby doubling the hysteria of its passengers. The man-made pond deceived the innocent spectator who contemplated riding the rails above it, for however beautifully landscaped the pond might have been, one found it difficult to overlook the shrieks reverberating above it. The structure was a daunting sight. It was menacing, yet inviting for those brave enough to ride it.

Tugging my arm, my older brother taunted me, trying to get me to join him on the ride. The more he insisted, the more I retreated. Finally, my mother told him to leave me alone. I found a lemonade stand across from the ride and much preferred to quietly sip the perfect blend of tart sweetness while watching my brother wildly scream with exhilaration. Several times while leaning on the fence intently watching the drama play out, I saw people's keys or coins fall into the pond, never to be returned. Suckers.

Two years later, I was a middle school student with books under my arm, slamming my locker and walking down crowded hallways to my next class. When asked by my two closest girlfriends if I would like to join them on a trip to Knott's Berry Farm, I didn't hesitate. Once there, they led the way and headed straight for the Corkscrew. I followed as we chatted about school and boys. I hardly glanced at the structure above me as we waited in line for our turn. I climbed in, pushed the restraint bar to my lap and gripped the black rubber padding. As we were pulled upward, the climb began. The view was great, but it quickly disappeared as we were jerked around and turned upside down, our bodies thrown from side to side. I remained silent as my riding companion screamed her head off.

As we departed the Corkscrew, my friend told the others that I was as cool as a cucumber through the whole ride. I was the object of unjustified admiration. What had—two years earlier—been an inner struggle of eagerness versus fear was now reduced to only a footnote in a day's activities at Knott's Berry Farm.

As it was with my Corkscrew ride, the starting point of adoption is all about readiness. What seems impossible at one point in time may be quite simple at another. The trick is to recognize the importance of readiness when approaching the platform of adoption.

Joel didn't immediately jump on board the day I shared my calling to adopt with him. During this frustrating time waiting for my husband to "take the ride" with me, my mind continued to return to the story of Mary, Jesus's mother. She answered the ultimate call to bear the savior in her womb, and her husband was not on board initially either. Joseph was left in the dust for a while, thinking that Mary had been unfaithful. I was encouraged that eventually God sent an angel to Joseph and told him that Mary 's pregnancy was, in fact, the work of the Lord. Trust me, many times I impatiently pleaded with the Lord to just send Gabriel down in a dream so that Joel would be assured that his wife was not completely crazy!

Patience is not my strong suit. While I knew it was critical to be united in our adoption plan, I had to repress my resolute determination and raw emotions to allow for civilized discussion on the topic. Joel is a faithful follower of the Lord, and I had confidence he would come around. Yet I felt a pressure to convince and continue to readdress the issue in order to gain his support. During those conversations, Joel presented his objections. He wondered if I was simply having an emotional reaction to the situation with Ava and whether my passion and enthusiasm about adoption would pass. From his perspective, adoption meant spending a lot of money for the experience of bringing the unknown into his perfect family. He had two wonderful children and a wife he loved very much. An unexpected idea had now invaded this sanctity and was overshadowing every bit of reason he possessed. He was torn between his love for me and his sense of reason. After all, his life was vested in evidence and irrefutable logic. How could I expect him to turn over a new leaf and to accept something that at first seemed so illogical?

It wasn't long before the Air Force interceded in a way that extended his ability to contemplate for a period of five months. Joel was deployed to the Middle East. At first, I was concerned that I was losing ground through our inability to face the pressing adoption discussion together. Then, one morning after Joel had left, I awoke with the feeling that maybe the Lord and the Air Force were in cahoots to create a five-month distraction for Joel. When he left for his deployment, he was still resistant. It was my turn to wait and, by so doing, allow time for the Lord to break down Joel's many, valid concerns. In the meantime, my children and I endured a cold and quite snowy Idaho winter.

Shortly after Joel returned from his deployment to the Middle East, we enjoyed a pizza lunch at the Base Exchange food court together—a romantic getaway from the chatter of our children. He shared that he had done a lot of thinking and praying while he was away, and he was willing to support me. He had many concerns about adopting: the impact on our other two children, how old he would be at our child's high school graduation, the reality that we would have less freedom and the factor of finances. Nevertheless, he said, "We are a team. We have always been a team. If the Lord has called you in this way, then he has called me too." Yes! We were past the turnstile and climbing aboard!

What initially appeared to be a Mount Everest-sized problem seemed to have evaporated without significant persuasion. As was true with the Corkscrew ride, it was simply a matter of readiness. I knew that my husband's commitment was subject to further doubt, but we were united as we proceeded with a plan to adopt.

In the midst of our struggle to be united, the scripture Jeremiah 50:4 provided clarity: "In those days, at that time," declares the LORD, "the people of Israel and the people of Judah together will go in tears to seek the LORD their God." The focal point of this verse is that the Israelites and people of Judah, *together,* went to seek the Lord. They shared their brokenness with the Lord in sorrow and also rejoiced in the mercy of God. They were about to set off on a journey to return to their own country after being in bondage and captivity for such a long time. As we prepared to set out on our adoption journey, it became important that we prayed *together* about this calling.

Another passage that punctuated the need for unification in our approach was Ephesians 4:3: "The Holy Spirit makes you one in every way. So try your best to remain as one. Let peace keep you together." This was one of my hardest struggles, being confident enough that the Lord would work in Joel's heart that I could feel peace and not pressure to change his mind. No amount of debate or discussion was going to be effective. There were many times I felt myself swallow my words and pray for the Lord to take over. It needed to be the work of the Holy Spirit in Joel's heart that nudged him to get on board. Arguments, dissension and friction in our relationship is not what the Lord intended to create with this calling, that I knew.

Trusting in the Lord requires patience in His ways. Seek to be united in your approach, and have patience in His ways as the Lord readies you and your family for adoption.

Scripture

Jeremiah 50:4
"In those days, at that time," declares the LORD, "the people of Israel and the people of Judah together will go in tears to seek the LORD their God."

Ephesians 4:3
The Holy Spirit makes you one in every way. So try your best to remain as one. Let peace keep you together.

Thoughts Along the Way

If you are feeling like your quest for adoption is one-sided, what do you feel your role is in helping your spouse/partner get "on board?"

Write a prayer, preferably *together*, sharing your brokenness with the Lord and rejoicing in His mercy.

3

THIS WAY

The Why of Hardship

A few months after Joel returned from the Middle East, we moved from Idaho to Alabama. Montgomery would be our seventh assignment in the military, so I Ziploc-bagged the kitchen utensils, set aside the family photo albums in the Do Not Pack pile, and watched three burly men pack up and pull away with all our worldly belongings. We then loaded up our two cars and caravanned across the country with two kids, two guinea pigs, and a venti Starbucks coffee for me.

Moving is the ultimate reminder of what you actually need in life. Everything in those two cars—my husband, my children, their blankets, some food (and the photo albums, which really equate to memories)—was all I needed. The other 16,000 pounds of stuff was unnecessary. It was freeing, even briefly, to be in between houses. As we pressed forward toward Alabama, my mind rewound.

The summer prior to my senior year at Pepperdine University, I was selected to attend the National Psychological Institute of Washington D.C. for a summer of specialized study in psychology. Upon my arrival at the Georgetown dormitory,

Darnell Hall, I met a girl in the bathroom while washing my hands. Rachel and I were both in D.C. as interns, although she was there to intern for a congressman on Capital Hill. Rachel invited me to play softball with her congressman's office the next evening on the Capital Hill Mall. Since I knew not a single person in D.C., I quickly accepted. My bathroom buddy told me to meet her in the Cannon Congress building. With a smartphone in hand, this might have been an easier task. However my summer in D.C. (1994) pre-dated the invention of the iPhone, so I carefully unfolded and studied a map of D.C. I started my trek first by taking the bus down Pennsylvania Avenue, then transferred to the subway that dumped me at Capitol South metro stop. Riding up the escalator, the gigantic white congressional building slowly came into view, with the Capitol rotunda as the backdrop to this breathtaking sight. I was in awe. Unbeknownst to me, this would be the stage where I would meet my husband-to-be.

I clicked along the white marble hallway in my heels (with tennis shoes in my backpack), and entered in the congressman's office. My bubbly bathroom acquaintance introduced me to fellow interns. The tall, blond, baby-faced Air Force Academy football player stood out immediately. On the lawn between the White House and the Washington Monument, our softball game ensued. I ran to first base on a ground ball, Joel made a grand slam and slid into home plate. After the game, we hung out and drank a beer to celebrate our win. Joel sat on the back of a wooden bench, laughing with his Air Jordan hat cocked slightly to the side. My eyes were fixed on him.

We exchanged letters that fall, and in December my father and I flew back East, exploring campuses for my first year of graduate study. During the trip, my dad—who was as down-to-earth as one could get—listened to my incessant chatter about Joel. He finally said, "You are making a mistake looking to go to graduate school. If what you say about this guy is true, my advice is to go to wherever he is. Upon his graduation, the Air Force will send him to his first assignment. You go to him there." This came from a gray- haired fellow with a doctorate from USC. His advice flew in the face of the high regard my father had for academics. It was completely out of character and, because it was so unlike him, the merit of his advice could not be ignored. So it was that I postponed my studies in favor of being with Joel after graduation. I learned that his first assignment would be to Intelligence School in San Angelo, Texas.

That was assignment number one, and I was now entertaining two children in a cross-country road trip to assignment number seven. I had withstood earthquakes growing up in California, experienced hurricanes in Hawaii and trudged through snowstorms living in Heidelberg, Germany during my year abroad in college. But tornadoes sent a pang of fear through my entire body.

I prepped myself by watching *Twister* and stopped off at the Wizard of Oz Museum in Kansas on our cross-country road trip to Alabama. Joel jokes with me that I become a self-proclaimed expert in certain professional areas. At distinct points in our marriage, I have been a doctor or a botanist, and now I was a meteorologist extraordinaire. On the first Wednesday of each month, when the practice tornado sirens sounded in our neighborhood, the kids and I took action. We raced to our shelter under the stairs and reviewed our emergency plans for withstanding a real twister. Fortunately, our house was never struck that year. Unfortunately, my health took a hit instead, and I spiraled into my own destructive swirl.

I spent the majority of that year on my couch, curled up with menstrual cramps and unstoppable bleeding. As time went by, my strength ebbed until I became completely devoid of energy. The constant pain sapped my vitality until I was hardly conscious. The raging fibroid plus poor medical care left me in a situation in which the most I could do was drag myself from the bed to the bathroom. On our frequent trips to the base hospital, I was mystified by the young men in white coats addressed by the nurses as doctors. These were pubescent interns who had, just yesterday, shaved for the first time. The captain bars worn on their uniform lapels were deceptive advertising. With ballpoint pens protruding from their white coat breast pockets and stethoscopes dangling from their necks, they imitated experience. The varying doctors listened to my complaints with half-closed eyes, then scratched out a prescription for pills on a printed pad and checked their watches to be sure they would not miss happy hour at the Officers' Club. At every visit Joel fumed, but we knew it did little good in the Air Force's bureaucracy of health care.

I did not know who to feel most sorry for, Joel or myself. Every moment he was home he fretted over me, bringing me pills, water and juice. In an effort to replenish the blood I was losing he barbequed steaks and fed me spinach. His days playing football for the Air Force Academy served him well, as one night he had to carry me to the car for yet another emergency room visit. He never spoke of how his worry affected his attentiveness at Air Command Staff College, but I imagine my husband's stellar academic focus may have been clouded.

After six months of hormone alterations and various procedures, I made the decision to end my womanly struggles and have a hysterectomy. While this seems like a big decision, and at the time I was fairly young for such action (I was 35 years old), continuing to be sick with two kids to care for was not an option. To make a long story short, I drove into Alabama with a uterus and drove out of Alabama (9 months later) without one.

By this point, almost two years had passed since the Lord called us to adopt. That's the thing about a calling: God's will does not fade. His persistence is endless.

Despite my physical problems I still heard His words breaking through the mist of pain just as clear as that day on the old country road: "You will adopt one of mine." That year in Alabama turned out to be one of the hardest years of my life. I am not an easy patient (just ask Joel).

Even with many miles of space and time between me and my year of illness in Alabama, the question of *why* haunted me. Why the fibroid? Why the pain? Why a hysterectomy?

On a crisp fall morning run, the Lord answered my *why*. He reminded me of this scripture, "Your eyes saw me before I was put together. And all the days of my life were written in your book before any of them came to be." (Psalm 139:16) When God called us to adopt, He knew the road ahead. He knew that I would have health issues that would present me with difficult decisions. Being the loving God, the all-powerful God, the provider of all things good, He intervened well *before* my time of trial to give me direction and purpose. He brought the needs of an unborn child and whispered her soul into my heart in Idaho on that old country road. The Lord's calling made my hysterectomy decision an easy one. Biological childbirth was now an impossibility, a road I could no longer travel or debate with my husband. His plan was taking shape. I don't blame God for that awful year. Instead, I thank Him for providing me with clear markers, like big flashing arrows pointing *This Way*.

Scripture

Psalm 139:16
Your eyes saw me before I was put together. And all the days of my life were written in your book before any of them came to be.

Thoughts Along the Way

Is there an episode in your life about which you struggle to understand the *why*? Do you have any resolution? If so, write down your understanding of the *why*.

If not, pray for patience in God revealing the why. Sometimes we may never understand the *why* of hardship. But we can lean on the Lord and trust that he knows and is in charge.

4

PEACE PATIENCE TRUST

Winning at the Waiting Game

My kitchen in Alabama was a Southern belle, clothed in all-white cabinets and a sunshine yellow trim. She stood adjacent to the entryway and greeted all with a warm and gracious, Daryl Hannah in *Steel Magnolias* welcome. Insert our little family of four, and we might as well have been on the cover of Southern Living. After a long day at school and work, we sat down at the rectangular, white, tiled table to eat a chicken dinner. But something was out of place; something was missing. Ah yes…my clothes.

Uncontrollable hot flashes had reduced my in-house attire to bare basics—undies and a bra. There were no guests invited to the England's during that period of time! In an effort to fight my uterine fibroid and stop the bleeding that put me on the edge of needing a blood transfusion, the doctor prescribed a medication that completely shut down all hormones and put me into full-blown menopause. I had no idea how big a role my hormones played in my physical and emotional health until I had none!

That night, I sat at the table with sweat pooling between my bare legs and the wooden chair, half-heartedly eating my chicken breast, when all I really wanted to do was pull a popsicle out of the freezer and stick it in my bra. But had I done that, my preschooler would have wanted a Popsicle instead of his chicken, and the nutritious dinner I had cooked would have ended up in the trash.

In silent self-talk, I started going down the "boo hoo me" road. It had been more than two years since the Lord had called us to adopt. Since that time, Joel deployed, we moved to Alabama and I got sick. In a few short months we would be facing another move, this time to Maryland. We had made no progress in the adoption direction. In fact, all I had done was sit on the couch and make ER visits as the victim of a uterine fibroid. Sliding on my chair half-naked at the dinner table, I could not have been further from where I initially envisioned myself after receiving that country-road calling. I wondered why the Lord would direct such action and then make it nearly impossible to attain?

As I trudged through thoughts, my mind suddenly shifted gears. The mantra "peace, patience, trust" popped up like the emergency concrete barrier on the military base that aims to stop terrorists from ramming the gates. At that moment, I reminded myself to take a deep breath and have peace that this adoption *would* happen. I willed myself to have patience in the Lord's plan. I said a silent prayer to the Lord: "I trust You." That mantra, "peace, patience, trust" got me through those first four years of waiting to take solid action.

Adoption takes time, and time was one of my biggest concerns. It was usually the first topic I addressed in informational adoption meetings, "...and how long does that take?" As it turned out, once we made the decision to adopt via independent adoption, it was exactly one year (almost to the day) that our daughter was born. The longest part of the process involved Joel and I getting to the same spot and then making the decision about which adoption route was best for us.

My practical advice is to use this time for preparation. Here are a few suggestions:

- Keep a journal of your thoughts and emotions.
- Seek the Lord and His word.
  - ✓ Join a small group.
  - ✓ Participate in a Bible study.
  - ✓ Spend time alone in worship (listen to Christian music, take a quiet hike, wake up early and watch the sunrise).
  - ✓ Pray and memorize scripture.
- Work to improve your mental and physical health.
  - ✓ Take Yoga or try Pilates.
  - ✓ Find a workout that suits you (running, aerobics, swimming, etc.).
- Talk to a counselor and work through any tough issues that may raise their ugly heads when you delve into the home study process.
- Take a FUN trip with your spouse.
- Take a course on child development.
- Start a new hobby.

God knows us. In His word He addresses that His plan for you may feel slow in coming. Check out Habakkuk 2:3: "For it is not yet time for it to come true. The time is coming in a hurry, and it will come true. If you think it is slow in coming, wait for it. For it will happen for sure, and it will not wait." There is a lot to do while you wait. Make the most of this time.

Waiting is tough, though. The Jews of the Old Testament can relate. God had promised a new covenant with his people that the Messiah would come. But they had to wait 400 years on the Lord's plan.

Here is how this went down. In Malachi 3:1, which was written around 450 BC, the Lord spoke, "Look! I am sending my messenger, and he will prepare the way before me." God was alerting His people to watch out for John the Baptist. But then generations waited and waited. Finally, after 400 years of God not saying anything (no prophets, no angels) He showed up to fulfill that promise.

An angel appeared to Zachariah and told him he is to have a child named John. "He will be a man with the spirit and power of Elijah. He will prepare the people for the coming of the Lord," Luke 1:17. Yep, the Jews waited 400 years. The key here is that not *ever* has one of God's promises in the Bible not come to fruition. Joshua drove this point home, "You know with all your heart and soul that not one of all the good promises the Lord your God gave you has failed. Every promise has been fulfilled; not one has failed." (Joshua 23:14)

While human promises may disappoint, God's word is foolproof. This is what God promises you:

- He will always work for good in your life. (Romans 8:28)
- He will never leave you. (Hebrews 13:5)
- He will take away your fear. (Psalm 34:4)

What He doesn't promise is that you will never experience pain or that adoption will be easy. One way to set yourself up for success is to manage your expectations according to the Lord's word.

Do you expect the Lord to be a part of this adoption? Do you expect that the Lord can navigate you through the bumps on this road to adoption? Do you expect the Lord to strengthen your marriage, your family and your faith through this process? Do you expect that at the end of this process, you will be holding your child?

One scripture I memorized that was extremely helpful was Philippians 4:4-7. "Rejoice in the Lord always. I will say it again: Rejoice! Let your gentleness be evident to all. The Lord is near. Do not be anxious about anything, but in every situation, by prayer and petition, with thanksgiving, present your requests to God. And the peace of God, which transcends all understanding, will guard your hearts and your minds in Christ Jesus." That is one scripture to commit to memory!

Enjoy where you are right now. Even if you're sweating and naked at the dinner table, there is laughter to be had. Trusting that you are where you are supposed to be will bring peace. Will yourself to have patience with the process. Trust that the Lord is working while you're waiting. His timing is perfect!

Scripture

Habakkuk 2:3 (NLV)
For it is not yet time for it to come true. The time is coming in a hurry, and it will come true. If you think it is slow in coming, wait for it. For it will happen for sure, and it will not wait.

Malachi 3:1 (MSG)
Look! I am sending my messenger, and he will prepare the way before me.

Luke 1:17 (NLT)
He will be a man with the spirit and power of Elijah. He will prepare the people for the coming of the Lord.

Joshua 23:14
You know with all your heart and soul that not one of all the good promises the LORD your God gave you has failed. Every promise has been fulfilled; not one has failed.

Romans 8:28
And we know that in all things God works for the good of those who love him, who have been called according to his purpose.

Hebrews 13:5
Never will I leave you; never will I forsake you.

Psalms 34:4 (NKJV)
I sought the Lord, and He heard me, and delivered me from all my fears.

Philippians 4:4-7
Rejoice in the Lord always. I will say it again: Rejoice! Let your gentleness be evident to all. The Lord is near. Do not be anxious about anything, but in every situation, by prayer and petition, with thanksgiving, present your requests to God. And the peace of God, which transcends all understanding, will guard your hearts and your minds in Christ Jesus.

Thoughts Along the Way

Write Peace, Patience, Trust on a note card, your smartphone notes or even a chalkboard in your kitchen. Keep them close at hand, and look at them often.

5

ON THE BANK

Overcoming Doubt

I sat in the passenger seat with Joel at the wheel. As we approached Richmond, Virginia, I twisted in my seat to check on Alex and Kelsey in the back. Plugged into their headphones, they were momentarily silent.

"I feel like I can breathe again," I said in reference to leaving Montgomery, the scene of so much personal agony. As we drove north toward Maryland for yet another assignment, I was full of hope and optimism.

There is a concept in psychology known as state-dependent memory. Basically, it explains how your memory tends to recall events that are consistent with your current mood. Predictably, my happy and elevated mood transported my mind across the Pacific Ocean to paradise. "Remember the time in Hawaii," I reminisced with Joel about our carefree island life. For hours on that drive we laughed and relished the memories of our special time on the island of Oahu.

Joel's assignment had been to the Joint Intelligence Center of the Pacific on Pearl Harbor. With a smile on my face I remembered my morning runs at the opening to Pearl Harbor while watching the delighted fish peck at algae on the rocks; eating shaved ice at Island Snow in Kailua; sailing lessons with my best friend; all-day turtle watching with Joel on our North Shore beach; and surfing Waikiki. We played hard, but we also worked hard those three years. I was studying to get my Master's Degree at the University of Hawaii, and Joel started his day on the early shift (3:00 a.m. Hawaii time). Our arduous efforts paid off, Joel was accepted to law school at the University of Arizona Law School and I received my Master's Degree and began work as a mental health therapist for children and teens.

Now the kids began to argue in the back seat, *Finding Nemo* had ended, and our trip down memory lane jerked to an abrupt halt. We stayed at the Holiday Inn that night. The kids played shark—Alex was Bruce from *Nemo* at the indoor pool. We all slept soundly in the knowledge that the next day's drive would take us to our new house in Crofton, Maryland.

I knew that once we were settled we would face the topic of adoption. The furniture arrived, Joel took up his duties at Fort Meade and the kids opened their books at Crofton Elementary school. I did the groundwork to begin teaching psychology at the community college, and each of us fell into a lifestyle that was both challenging and rewarding. At this point, the Lord's words had been burned into my consciousness, and I had no reservations about letting my husband know what I was thinking.

Joel and I attended several adoption meetings and learned that the list of tasks stretched into the unknown. The requirements were stringent and the twists and turns in the process made us dizzy with information overload. The more Joel delved into the details of the process, the more ominous the adoption became. He saw the potential problems piling up, one after another. As one was overcome, two others appeared.

His misgivings were logically justified, but I saw only the other side of the rainbow, while he was caught in the torrent of rain.

One afternoon as we sat on the front deck of our house with the enormous adoption binder unfolded in front of us, Joel—still overwhelmed with doubt—shared his hesitancies and I once again, stood steadfast in my belief that the Lord would work out the details. Frustrated, Joel stood up and walked away saying that he needed to take a breather. I watched as his military strides resembled a one-man attack on an imaginary enemy.

Two hours passed, and I was becoming worried. Just about the time I was ready to gather the kids to go out on a search mission, his muddy feet led him in the back door. He had a look on his face that communicated that something big had happened. Between breaths, he relayed to me how he had walked to the local pond behind our house and prayed. What he shared with me next made my heart leap. Beside the pond, the Lord penetrated his crust of reason by pointing a finger at the real reason for his fear of adoption. With the correction, guidance and the assurance that only the Lord could give, Joel came back ready. The Holy Spirit to whom I had prayed to melt and mold Joel's heart arrived that day.

On the banks of that pond, God revealed to him three critical truths. The first truth was that the roots of most of his concerns were selfish. (This is Joel's explanation, not mine.) The Lord illustrated that Joel's misgivings stemmed from an outlay of money, energy and time. These were all earthly concerns that the Lord gently corrected. While I was not present on the bank of the pond, I know that the Lord must have been as unequivocal with Joel as he had been with me because the burden of worry was fully drowned by the words of the Lord, and it never resurfaced.

The second truth highlighted the error in Joel's approach. Up until that point, he relied on his analytical legal mind to make decisions. Bring on the evidence, and the right choice would depend upon the weight of evidence. But on the banks of that mossy pond, the Lord directed my husband to cast out the evidence, remove the straitjacket of illusionary logic and take on the mantel of faith. Fear will vanish when one trusts the Lord to be the pathfinder. Be guided by His direction, and use one's mind to set into motion His desires.

Lastly, He revealed a truth about love. There were lingering questions that not even my most careful wording could answer. My husband has been blessed with an enormous intellect. His ability to see any problem not apparent to me was a gift—a warning of a subtle, hidden problem I could not visualize. The questions that lurked just beneath the surface like floating mines were:

- *Do we have in us the ability to love our adopted child with the same fervor with which we love our biological children?*
- *Will we have time to provide our best efforts to a child who will perhaps need more love than we believe we can give?*
- *If we are able to give an abundance of love to our adopted child, will that love be subtracted from the love that we would otherwise give our biological children?*

The revelation of truth that God presented to Joel that day was this: God enables in us the capacity to love like He loves. The assumption that one has a finite amount of love is an untrue one. God's love is infinite. We are made in His image. Ephesians 3:18: "May you have power with all God's people to understand Christ's love. May you know how wide and long and high and deep it is." There are no outer dimensions to love, no boundaries. Like air rushing into a vacuum, love expands as the demand for it expands. The place where Joel thought a problem existed turned out to be nothing more than a mirage.

Even though at an earlier point in our adoption quest we had resolved to march shoulder-to-shoulder through the adoption process, this resolution was made with a certain degree of naivety. Now, with concrete information in front of him, Joel committed to translating the Lord's calling into positive action, and our first step would be deciding which adoption route to take. On the bank of the pond the Lord pushed forward three crucial truths that erased, in one stroke, the earthly doubts that hindered the acceptance of our calling.

Scripture

Ephesians 3:18 (NIRV)
May you have power with all God's people to understand Christ's love. May you know how wide and long and high and deep it is.

Thoughts Along the Way

Are you and your spouse all-in? What are some doubts that are still lingering for you?

Maybe you have some of the same doubts Joel had or others we did not consider. Studying the Word of God may bring needed answers. Make a commitment to read His word daily.

6

THE EDGE

Choosing a Path and Taking the Dive

On a sweltering, late summer day in Maryland, I walked out the door and immediately recognized the futility of the past hour I had spent getting ready. My sleek, blown-dry, straightened locks breathed in the wet air and *poof*-turned into a total ball of frizz. I was taking the Metro to the Women of Faith conference at the Verizon Center in downtown Washington D.C., seeking quality time with the Lord and wanting to gain some wisdom from strong, Godly women. I accomplished both of these goals, but God showed up in an unexpected way as well.

During our lunch break, I wandered outside to get something to eat. I began sweating the minute I stepped outside so I sought the closest restaurant without a line. A few months earlier, Joel had surprised me with a Valentine's Day scavenger hunt at the National Gallery of American Art, which is located directly across the street from the Verizon Center, and there was a great little cafeteria in the museum's atrium. I ducked into the air-conditioned museum and quickly scarfed down a sandwich so that I could pass the uniformed guard and browse the famed art collection. He patiently waited for me to jam the last bite into my mouth and then waved me through.

I walked slowly from exhibit to exhibit and came upon a hall dedicated to the work of Norman Rockwell. As a fan of the master of human nature and unsurpassed oil painter of the human condition, I slowed my pace as I entered the darkened corridor. I meandered down the first hallway and approached a painting that immediately caught my attention. It was me. I mean, it was not *me*, but it could have been! The painting depicts a young child in a bathing suit, crouched on all fours on a wooden diving board. He had crawled out to the edge, peering just over the high dive, his eyes wide with fear. The boy's white-knuckle grip on the edge of the board punctuates his panic, as he considers his impending choice. Anyone observing his expression can likely relate to the juxtaposition of fear and determination. Through his art, Norman Rockwell was holding a mirror to my emotions when it came to the adoption.

The Lord revealed my fears through Rockwell's painting but also normalized my emotions. I think that perhaps anyone who has ever stood at the edge of something significant experiences feelings similar to the boy on the high dive; it's natural for anxiety to accompany courage.

As I exited the museum down the grand marble steps, I realized that God had transformed my fear into excitement. He had reminded me that the moment you realize you are standing on the edge is also the point at which something great is likely to begin.

Have you ever jumped off a high dive? There was one at our community pool, and while it does not look terribly high from below, once you climb the stairs and walk out on the platform, it is much more foreboding. There is a decisive moment in which you must intentionally *make* your feet leave the edge. And that is a scary moment.

You may be at the critical point at which you and your spouse need to decide which route to take with your adoption. This decision is overwhelming, and it should be! It is a critical fork in the road that requires defining one's own needs and then marrying those needs to the type of adoption that best matches them. Whether you choose to partner with an agency or an independent adoption lawyer (like we did) this point in your journey deserves ample thought and discussion.

This particular juncture in the adoption process is both time-consuming and necessary. Books, Web searches, informational meetings and conversations with other adoptive parents may be beneficial resources during this decision-making process. The good news is that this decision point is in your hands.

We began information gathering by going to agency meetings with speakers who had expertise in one or more aspects of adoption. Needless to say, two school-age children, obligations as an Air Force spouse and part-time work as a college instructor made attending these meetings a strain on our already tight schedule. Joel and I peeled ourselves away from our two children, hired a babysitter and after long workdays sat through adoption seminars. Once we had attended a few agency-based sessions, we began to get the hang of these get-togethers. The routine was to sit on uncomfortable folding chairs with our binder, receive a few handouts and an agency pen. Then we were fire-hosed with information, including numerous hoops to be jumped through and countless hours of mandatory parenting training. Thankfully, we were also offered a free chocolate chip cookie and cup of coffee!

The Lord wants you to hear this, "Trust in the LORD with all your heart and do not lean on your own understanding. In all your ways acknowledge Him and He will make your paths straight." (Proverbs 3:5-6) As you sift through the mountains of information and various adoption options, trust that He will guide your way.

Here is a tip: keep all of the agency pens that you unwittingly collect. Consider them souvenirs from this trip. After all is said and done—and it will be sooner rather than later—you will randomly pull out one of those pens to sign your child's field trip form and smile fondly.

Scripture

Proverbs 3:5-6 (NASB)
Trust in the LORD with all your heart and do not lean on your own understanding. In all your ways acknowledge Him and He will make your paths straight.

Thoughts Along the Way

Consider how you would approach a high-dive. Would you charge up the stairs and launch off, or would there be trepidation in your steps, followed by kneeling down to peer over? How do you think your typical approach to scary scenarios might affect your decision-making during the adoption process?

Keep in mind that there is not a good or bad personality type; the key is to understand yourself well enough that you can identify your tendencies and move past any fears with the assurances from our Lord.

7

JOHNNIE WALKER RED MOMENTS

Ruling Out Options and Zeroing In

Adoption agency pen in hand, I was poised to take notes at yet another informational adoption meeting. I observed the speaker, a social worker with streaks of gray running through her hair. I was comforted by her appearance, hoping to learn from her seasoned experience with adoption. The evening's topic was international adoption.

I begin taking copious notes about age requirements for adoptive parents (we immediately crossed off Korea; we were too old). I noted the varying countries' policies regarding the average age of adoptive children as well as their parameters when it came to children's disabilities. I took notes and more notes, crossed large X's through a few countries and circled others. I like tangible facts, and I felt good about this meeting.

The social worker began to tell stories, starting with, "This one time…" or, "The sweetest family…" From Russia to Korea and Guatemala to Ethiopia, she was familiar with the customs and hidden cultural nuances that could serve as pitfalls for adoptive families who weren't properly educated.

She then described a family that was "wholly unprepared" for their trip to Russia to pick up their daughter. Their first error was in not having thousands of dollars on hand in small bills, at all times in anticipation of "the call" from the agency letting them know that it was time to pick up their daughter. Sure enough, "the call" came on a Saturday night, and they were unable to access their bank. They were warned that without a large amount of cash, it would be virtually impossible to wind their way through the mounds of red tape once in Russia. Frantic, they tapped every resource available to them and were able to gather the necessary money. On the way to the airport, however, they received a call from a representative of the adoption agency stating that the judge had a specific request. He didn't want money; he wanted two bottles of Johnnie Walker Red whiskey. Once again, the couple danced the dance, this time in order to find the proper label on a bottle of alcohol. I envisioned the nervous, soon-to-be first-time mother running into the shady, 24-hour liquor store near the airport, stashing two bottles of whiskey into her neatly packed diaper bag and heading to Russia to pick up their daughter. And so the story went, through the bureaucratic maze that was apparently completely normal for the Russian adoption experience.

The disparity between our idyllic picture of adoption and the picture of a frantic couple gathering cash and stashing bottles of whiskey in preparation for their adoption was wide enough for us to consider alternative options. Our biggest concerns in the area of international option were the added bureaucracy, longer wait times for a child and larger financial commitment.

Having said that, I want to emphasize that there is a route that makes sense for everyone, and international adoption is a wonderful adoption choice for many. God's children are God's children, regardless of where they are born. Some of the most desperate conditions for children are found outside the United States where resources are scarce. There are organizations, like Steven Curtis Chapman's Show Hope, whose mission is "restoring the hope of a family to orphans in distress." (*ShowHope.org*) Show Hope provides grants to adopting families (both international and domestic) and has built and manages medical facilities in China to treat orphans with severe medical conditions. The work of this organization is truly the hand of the Lord on earth.

You may hear of adoption stories in which the outcomes did not meet the perfect glass-slipper-fit expectations. When I initially received the calling to adopt, I shared my enthusiasm with a pastor. Expecting a "Hallelujah and hands-raised" response I was shocked when his response was, instead, a stiff-arm warning. He provided a personal experience in which he had counseled a church member who adopted and bumped into unforeseen behavioral and emotional hurdles with their adopted child. I believe my pastor's comments were intended to provide a fair picture, not a fairy-tale version, of adoption. Yet I was upset, even angry, at his comments. Why would he squelch my excitement and thirst for adoption through this story of struggle? I did not allow these comments to hinder my pursuit, or lessen God's will in our lives. I moved ahead, knowing that there were inherent risks in adoption, but chose to stay focused on the countless stories of miraculous healing, heart-tugging love, and glorious grace in adoption. The one story that I urge you to keep on the forefront of your mind is from Matthew 25:40:

> "When the Son of Man comes in his glory, and all the angels with him, he will sit on his glorious throne. All the nations will be gathered before him, and he will separate the people one from another as a shepherd separates the sheep from the goats. He will put the sheep on his right and the goats on his left.

> "Then the King will say to those on his right, 'Come, you who are blessed by my Father; take your inheritance, the kingdom prepared for you since the crea-creation of the world. For I was hungry and you gave me something to eat, I was thirsty and you gave me something to drink, I was a stranger and you invited me in, I needed clothes and you clothed me, I was sick and you looked after me, I was in prison and you came to visit me.'
>
> "Then the righteous will answer him, 'Lord, when did we see you hungry and feed you, or thirsty and give you something to drink? When did we see you a stranger and invite you in, or needing clothes and clothe you? When did we see you sick or in prison and go to visit you?'
>
> "The King will reply, 'Truly I tell you, whatever you did for one of the least of these brothers and sisters of mine, you did for me.'"

God did not promise that adoption would be easy, he does, however, urge us to care for the "least of these" whether that is in the U.S. or abroad.

While our choice was for a domestic adoption, I urge you to explore all options, carefully and judiciously weighing the pros and cons of each. One smart approach to your analysis will be to look at adoption trends. For example, in 2008 there were 17,416 international adoptions, but that number decreased significantly to 8,650 in 2012.[1] This fluctuation in numbers was mostly due to changes in foreign countries' agreements with the U.S. regarding adoption.

It is critical to do your homework *before* you sign on with a particular agency. A friend recently shared how she and her husband initially signed on with an adoption agency. However, they decided to change course after gaining more specific information regarding the wait time and processes involved. That shift on their adoption path cost them $10,000.

While each informational session helped us hone in on the best path for our adoption, we were still not convinced of a single approach that was a good fit for our circumstances. Little did we know, God was about to show up in one of my favorite places.

While at the salon getting my hair done (or, to be clear, colored since I was starting to get a bit of gray), I overheard a woman talking about adoption. My ears tuned in to her words. It seemed that she had a lawyer friend who specialized in adoption. I noted the man's name and telephone number on the back of the shop's business card. When my husband returned from work that day, I met him at the door. As a lawyer himself, he readily agreed to meet with the adoption lawyer at a time that didn't interfere with his work schedule.

Joel had been reassigned from Fort Meade to the Pentagon, both of which were within reasonable distance from our home, meaning that we did not have to move and our efforts to adopt wouldn't be interrupted—at least not for another two years.

I called the law office of Mark McDermott and made an appointment for my husband and me to spend a few hours obtaining expert advice. That meeting ended up being the turning point in our quest to adopt a child. Being in the hands of an experienced lawyer allayed Joel's doubts by providing him with objective facts. I saw Mr. McDermott as an expert who knew the ins and outs of adoption so thoroughly that all of the previous meetings we had attended became inconsequential. This knowledgeable man made no attempt to recommend one avenue of adoption over another. Rather, he answered our questions, which came from the limited knowledge we'd gained reading and listening to others. At that initial meeting, we learned a great deal, and also gained comfort in knowing that we finally had a resource with whom we were completely comfortable.

Not only did we obtain information that would be critical in further decision-making moments, we were also informed of a non-profit group called Families For Private Adoption (www.FFPA.org).

Families For Private Adoption (FPA) provides biannual, comprehensive adoption workshops, a buddy system that pairs successful adoptive parents with prospective adoptive parents, and organizes social gatherings to share information and provide encouragement. FPA is not "selling" anything. Led by stellar professionals, it is simply a group of other prospective and experienced adoptive parents willing to help one another. And it works!

This group opened our eyes to a vista of previously unknown possibilities. Still, the thought of going it alone via an independent adoption seemed daunting. Being a military family, however, we couldn't be put on an agency wait list when our stay in any one particular state was temporary (two years at best). The amount of time that the adoption would take to complete was a key factor in our journey. With Joel's professional demands, my responsibilities as a community college psychology instructor, and our two children, we simply didn't have hours and hours to spend in the required parenting classes that are frequently a part of an agency process. This meant that we needed to move away from agencies and formal applications and move toward an option with more flexibility. We both realized that if we were to do this, we would need to lean on Mr. McDermott for continuous advice.

As it happened, FPA provided a full-day informational workshop on independent adoption soon after our meeting with Mr. McDermott. (By the way, the words "private adoption" and "independent adoption" are synonymous.) At last, our quest for knowledge was picking up speed; that one-day workshop set us up for success. Various speakers covered the steps involved in private adoption, and we received a comprehensive three-ring binder—the complete how-to guide to independent adoption. At the end of the meeting, the speaker said, "You now have everything you need to know to adopt." Walking to our car, each footstep solidified the approach that would work best for us: in-de-pen-dent, in-de-pen-dent (the story of *The Little Engine that Could* replayed in my head). We finally got up off of our hands and knees; it was time to jump.

Ardent attention and conscientious decision-making were critical during the next few months. I was already tired. There were many moments I asked the Lord to simply bring a baby to our door. Seriously, if it was His calling and will for our family to adopt, then why did I have to do all the legwork? I know it was a bit of a selfish prayer, but He could have made this process easier and quicker, right?

I was reminded of the parable of the sower. Jesus shared this story with his followers:

> "Then he told them many things in parables, saying: 'A farmer went out to sow his seed. As he was scattering the seed, some fell along the path, and the birds came and ate it up. Some fell on rocky places, where it did not have much soil. It sprang up quickly, because the soil was shallow. But when the sun came up, the plants were scorched, and they withered because they had no root. Other seed fell among thorns, which grew up and choked the plants. Still other seed fell on good soil, where it produced a crop—a hundred, sixty or thirty times what was sown. Whoever has ears, let them hear."

Through our adoption process, God was tilling and fertilizing the soil of our hearts, preparing and refining our family in order to make our home the perfect place for a child to flourish. The quick and easy route that I desired may well have landed us in a "rocky" or "thorny" place. Our laughter and tears, agreements and disagreements, defeats and triumphs, pros versus cons discussions enriched our marriage and family as we traveled down the adoption road.

After all the meetings and workshops, our own personal conclusion included a clear vote for independent adoption. Every story is different, but know this: the adoption route you choose will dictate the degree of complexity and number of hoops you may encounter. No matter which direction you choose, at some juncture there will be a realization that the adoption process you once imagined as "nice and neat check the box, pay your agency, create your profile and you're done" does not exist. You will, without doubt, have your own "Johnnie Walker Red" moment. The humorous stories born from the lengths to which you're willing to go for your child will be shared for years to come. One guarantee: it will be an amazing story.

Scripture

Matthew 25:31-40
"When the Son of Man comes in his glory, and all the angels with him, he will sit on his glorious throne. All the nations will be gathered before him, and he will separate the people one from another as a shepherd separates the sheep from the goats. He will put the sheep on his right and the goats on his left.

"Then the King will say to those on his right, 'Come, you who are blessed by my Father; take your inheritance, the kingdom prepared for you since the creation of the world. For I was hungry and you gave me something to eat, I was thirsty and you gave me something to drink, I was a stranger and you invited me in, I needed clothes and you clothed me, I was sick and you looked after me, I was in prison and you came to visit me.'

"Then the righteous will answer him, 'Lord, when did we see you hungry and feed you, or thirsty and give you something to drink? When did we see you a stranger and invite you in, or needing clothes and clothe you? When did we see you sick or in prison and go to visit you?'

"The King will reply, 'Truly I tell you, whatever you did for one of the least of these brothers and sisters of mine, you did for me.'"

Matthew 13:3-9
Then he told them many things in parables, saying: "A farmer went out to sow his seed. As he was scattering the seed, some fell along the path, and the birds came and ate it up. Some fell on rocky places, where it did not have much soil. It sprang up quickly, because the soil was shallow. But when the sun came up, the plants were scorched, and they withered because they had no root. Other seed fell among thorns, which grew up and choked the plants. Still other seed fell on good soil, where it produced a crop—a hundred, sixty or thirty times what was sown. Whoever has ears, let them hear."

Thoughts Along the Way

One effective way to spark constructive discussion about which adoption route to take is by completing a decision-making matrix. In creating your matrix, you will make a list of your unique considerations. Maybe it is the age of your adopted child, your desire for an open adoption, or financial considerations that are critical. Both you and your spouse assign weights and numbers to those considerations. There are many templates on the Web. I have included an example and directions below. While your final decision will not hinge on a single number value, it is helpful to see each other's differences and gain insight into each individual's desired direction.

Matrix Example

Criteria	**Cost 8 pts**	**Length of wait time 6 pts**	**Level of complexity 3 pts**	**Option for open adoption 2 pts**	**Age of child (Younger) 2 pts**	**Choice 2 pts**	**Level of Assistance 2 pts**	**TOTAL**
Adoption agency	2 X8 =16	2 X 6 =12	2 X3 =6	3 X2 =6	3 X2 =6	2 X2 =4	3 x2 =6	56
Indepen-dent Adoption	3 X8 =24	3 X6 =18	3 X3 =9	3 X2 =6	3 X2 =6	3 X2 =6	2 X2 =4	73
Interna-tional adoption	1 X8 =8	1 X6 =6	1 X3 =3	1 X2 =2	2 X2 =4	3 X2 =6	3 X2 =6	35
Foster Adoption	3 X8 =24	1 X6 =6	1 X3 =3	2 X2 =4	1 X2 =2	1 X2 =2	1 X2 =2	43

*Each person completes his or her own Matrix.

Matrix Instructions

Step 1-Together establish your adoption criterion (those things that are factors in considering adoption (cost, wait time, etc.).

Step 2-Individually complete the Matrix by first weighting each criterion, distributing 25 points.

Step 2-Assign numbers 1, 2, 3 in each adoption option (1 = negative impact, 2 = some impact, 3 = positive impact).

Step 3-Multiply each criterion by the assigned number.

Step 4-Add across each row for the total.

Step 5-Compare your matrices and discuss differences in numbers and create an action plan based on the discussion.

8

TANDEM

Taking the Back Seat

Nothing binds our family more than traditions. My Grandma and Papa were an integral part of our family life. They lived near Los Angeles but were often at our house, at the beach, attending weekend events and planning ritual excursions we took at dedicated times of year. It seemed that these getaways had always been a part of our family life; Snow Summit in the winter, Palm Desert in the spring and Catalina Island during the summer. What my grandparents had done as children, they passed on to my mother. What my mother had done as a child, she passed on to me. And what I had done as a kid, I now continue to do with my children. Although my Grandma and Papa have since passed on, their presence remains in our family as our getaways continue.

For four generations, our family has packed up the red wagon and beach dollies, loaded onto a barge (now a jet-powered catamaran) with 200 other beachgoers, and traveled 26 miles from the California coast to Catalina Island for a week of sun-soaked fun. The small port and quaint city of Avalon has few cars, and you can walk from one side of town to the other in less than 15 minutes. A waterfront, tiled pedestrian walkway is punctuated by fountains, an ice cream shop, boutiques and an old-fashioned taffy pull (with which I remain completely intrigued). I remember being a kid and playing Skeeball at the arcade, snorkeling in crystal-clear water with bright orange Garibaldi fish dancing in front of my facemask, and eating Grandma's tuna fish sandwiches on the beach. Every year, it brings me great joy to take my children to this special island.

One of Avalon's attractions is an old bike rental shop that specializes in tandem, two-seat bikes. A few years back, I decided to invite Alex, my then 10-year-old son, on an adventure with me. We walked to the other side of town to rent a tandem bike. Donning our helmets, I grabbed a map of the island, and we headed out. I peddled in front, and Alex balanced in back. Alex is my thinker. Even when he was a baby, I watched the wheels turn in his head while he was strapped into his car seat, staring out the window. Naturally, when he mounted the bike and realized his handles didn't turn, he was disturbed. I promised him that I knew what I was doing and recounted the many times I had done this as a child. Only 25 years earlier, my cousin and I had trekked the same pathways on a tandem bike. When I lost the Rock-Paper-Scissors game, she won the front seat and steering privileges. Putting my life in her hands was scary (sorry, Bridget, but it's true!). My life in *anyone* else's hands creates a distinct feeling of discomfort, to say the least.

Gaining speed through the salty ocean air, Alex shouted, "Where are we going, Mom?" I yelled to Alex, "Trust me."

I knew exactly where I was taking him. We passed the Casino and the Catalina Yacht Club.

Again, he asked, "Mom, where are we going?"

"Just pedal," I hollered back.

Since there were limited gears on the tandem, we had to pick up significant speed in order to make it up an impending steep hill. I hollered for Alex to pedal faster. Again, my cautious boy questioned why we had to go so fast.

"Come on, just pedal faster," I commanded.

He followed my lead. A brief moment later, he demanded, "Mom, just tell me where we are going."

I reached back, put my hand on his hand, and said, "Trust me, just keep pedaling and enjoy the ride, bud." I was breathing hard as I stood up in my seat to add my weight to the effort, and we crested the hill.

After just a few more minutes, a vista opened. There was a steep hillside on our left and the ocean on our right. A gentle curve formed a shallow cove with rocks along one side.

We rode along the cove. I kept my eyes forward, but the silence from behind confirmed Alex's enthusiasm for the scene I first knew as a child. I paused, put my feet down and enjoyed the moment with him. I was just as enthralled as he was to share in another world—a foreign domain of brightly colored fish. Gentle surface swells lazily pushed leafy kelp from side to side. The water forest swayed like trees in the wind. Voyeurs of an undisturbed world, completely free of human intervention, we stared at the small fish darting in and out of sight as they searched for invisible food.

"Was this worth the ride, Alex?" I asked.

He answered with a resounding, "Yes!"

Taking the back seat, as Alex did, is hard. It requires ultimate trust in your driver. Even when you put the Lord in the front seat of your adoption, you still may question the driver, "Where are we going?" Like I did, you may want to take your hand off the handle-bar grip and tug on the back of Jesus' robe, and ask, "Excuse me, but when will we meet our birth mom?" Followed by, "Who will be the child that will call me Mom?" As your impatience mounts, the wind of doubt whipping, you desire answers especially to the question of, "How long will this ride take, anyway?

Being okay with not being the driver is tough. The more work you put into the adoption, the more deeply entrenched you become, and the yearning to know answers tugs much more strongly on your heart. You must will yourself to hear the Lord's voice saying, "Just keep pedaling. Trust me." You must allow yourself to feel His encouraging touch, a reassuring pat on the hand as you ride together.

Without question, your adoption ride will be worth every bit of energy. Your ability to withstand the duration and difficulties that may arise hinges upon your understanding that you are on a tandem bike ride-with Jesus in the lead. His greatest desire is for you to trust Him and follow Him.

It is human nature to want to be in control. I attempted to bargain with the Lord, begged to switch seats so that I could steer for a little while. He denied my offer.

In Hebrews 11:8 we learn, "By faith Abraham, when called to go to a place he would later receive as his inheritance, obeyed and went, even though he did not know where he was going." That is the crux of adoption, *you have to be willing to go by faith and commit to completing the journey, even when you cannot see the destination.*

In time the Lord will reveal His master plan. Eventually, when you turn the corner, breathless and exhausted, you will hold a child in your arms and thank the driver for an incredible journey. All you have to do is pedal.

Scripture

Hebrews 11:8
By faith Abraham, when called to go to a place he would later receive as his inheritance, obeyed and went, even though he did not know where he was going.

Thoughts Along the Way

Describe a situation in which you had no control over the direction and/or outcome. What was your reaction? How did you successfully navigate that situation? Be specific!

By observing what has worked for you in the past, you can identify those tools and use them now and in the future.

9

YOUR NEW PART-TIME JOB

Carving Out Time for Adoption

With the exception of brief time periods between moves as well as directly before and after having a baby, I have worked. Whether counseling, consulting or teaching college courses, I've become a master at making the most of my time. Early mornings and late nights, plus the school carpool line have long been my 9-5. The driver's seat of my van is a functional office, and the front porch coffee table was converted to a desk that allowed me to prep for lectures, grade, document counseling sessions and consider interventions for clients.

So when our adoption attorney, Mark, matter-of-factly instructed us to "treat adoption like a part-time job," I spun into panic mode. He continued on, and I am sure he said many other wise words after those initial six, but I was oblivious, tumbled in a washing machine of thoughts.

"But wait," I thought, "I already have a part-time job. And two children. And volunteer obligations. And my kitchen is a mess…" While drowning in cynicism, I rewound to my Psychology 101 lecture on Beck's cognitive theory, where the value of recognizing irrational beliefs and replacing them with more logical, self-enhancing beliefs is emphasized. Even before Beck, Shakespeare wrote in *Hamlet*, "for there is nothing either good or bad, but thinking makes it so."[1] The power of thought has been proven to have an enormous impact on one's emotions and behavior. So I stopped "castastrophizing" and regrouped my thoughts.

I leaned on the Lord to help replace my negative filter with a positive one, shifting my focus to make the seemingly impossible possible. In Philippians 4:8, there is guidance about focus. It directs us to think about such things as, "whatever is true, whatever is noble, whatever is right, whatever is pure, whatever is lovely, whatever is admirable." If we put our mind in the right place, our actions will follow. My faith inspired self talk went something like this, "I've worked part-time most of my married life, so I am good at creating separation between work and family life. I have a supportive husband, a loving family and plenty of good friends. I can do this."

My plan was to carve out space in my schedule—at least part-time— and dedicate myself to our adoption. This required that, for starters, I not volunteer as much at my children's elementary school. I also set out specific days and times during the week when only adoption calls and work would be completed. While I couldn't stop working, I could trim away all unnecessary meetings and trainings. Joel also pitched in more with the kids and household duties, which helped tremendously. Joel's parents visited when they could, as did my father and mother. Any time our parents arrived on our doorstep, I sincerely welcomed them. They always alleviated the stress created from having to get too much completed in too little time.

Because independent adoption requires identifying a birth mom, the advertising component of the approach is time-intensive. However, every adoption route requires the completion of a home study, coordination with the agency on many levels and a profile for prospective birth mothers to review. All of these require significant time and effort. Mark's advice to consider it a part-time job, therefore, appropriately framed these tasks.

In Deuteronomy 1:11, it says, "May the LORD, the God of your ancestors, increase you a thousand times and bless you as he has promised!" I understand the context of this passage as a blessing Moses gave to the Israelites and a reminder of the favor God showed toward them. The words "increase you a thousand times" lodged in my brain. I chuckled at one point in our adoption thinking that it just might take 1,000 of me to successfully adopt. While my daydreams of cloning passed, my prayer to the Lord to help expand my time did not.

When others asked me to volunteer or attend certain functions, I found myself saying "no," kindly explaining that we were in the middle of an adoption. Not only were they understanding, they also asked how they could help. My kids had many more playdates that year with helpful friends. We had dinner brought to us by church members when we were in the thick of things. I found that people want to be a part of God's plan. It is grand and attractive and people are drawn to His light. Being honest and transparent about your time constraints during the adoption is necessary to completing the tasks.

Your new "part-time" job can easily morph into "full-time"; don't allow it to. Check the boxes, make the phone calls, put in a solid four hours' worth of consideration and discernment. Then, return to your spouse, watch a movie and relax, knowing that God is in the driver's seat.

Scripture

Philippians 4:8
Finally, brothers and sisters, whatever is true, whatever is noble, whatever is right, whatever is pure, whatever is lovely, whatever is admirable—if anything is excellent or praiseworthy—think about such things.

Deuteronomy 1:11
May the LORD, the God of your ancestors, increase you a thousand times and bless you as He has promised!

Thoughts Along the Way

Make a list of your Must-Dos and Can-Dos. The Must-Dos are those tasks in your life that are a requirement for the health, safety and wellness of yourself/spouse or family. The Can-Dos are those tasks that enrich your life but are not necessities. It is within the Can-Do section that you need to consider changes to accommodate your new "part-time" adoption job.

Remember, saying "No" or quitting a particular obligation does not mean you are a failure or are letting someone else down. You are on a mission that is of ultimate importance. Anyone who knows you well will not only understand but encourage you on this journey.

10

ILLUMINATION

Transformation Through His Light

After a fun (but long) summer in the Maryland humidity, the kids were finally back in school. The start of the school year is a frantic time, and I try as hard as I can to ensure that they have a smooth transition into their new grade—new backpacks, organized school supplies, snazzy new outfits and a treat in their lunches (topped off with a note of encouragement on a napkin). But then, that first-day-of-school morning arrives and, inevitably, despite my greatest efforts, there is an air of tension and some mini-disasters. This time, the eggs were brown and the zipper on the new backpack went off its rails. After drop-off for the start of 2nd and 5th grades for Alex and Kelsey respectively, I was completely exhausted—and it was only 8:30 a. m.!

At 8:31 a.m. I sat in my van and finally had a moment to think about something other than the summer essentials of sunscreen, mosquito spray and playdates. I relished in the fact that the day was mine, mine, all mine. What to do with all my fall freedom? Coffee. Bible.

About a mile away was a coffee shop called Caribou Coffee. It was a chilly start to the year, which is unusual in

Maryland, and I could feel a change of season coming. The crisp air was a welcome reprieve to the humid, sweaty summer. Many women had the same idea that day. The outside seating at Caribou was packed, but coffee in hand I pulled up a chair and plunked down, intending to stay for a while. It felt as though I hadn't sat for any significant period of time for at least three months. Facing the morning sun, I donned my sunglasses, sipped my coffee and let the cool breeze sweep over my body and the warm sun caress my face. There is something about the sun on my face that transforms me.

Have you ever seen a picture of (or been to) the Red Rocks of Sedona? I am not really a rock person. Striations, lime, mica—the interest just never took hold in geology class. However, these rocks are more than just geological wonders. The majestic red rocks jut up from the ground in towering, creative shapes. Living in Arizona, I have had the privilege of vacationing in Sedona. One of my favorite things to do is beat the sunrise and watch these rocks come to life. In the dark, the magnificent rock creations stand bland, and you awaken to simply the outline of grayish, black shapes. But as the sun begins to rise, you witness the truly awe-inspiring creation come to life. The rising sun illuminates the East face of the rock, and the shapes, angles, colors, and rocks themselves seem to come alive.

After this long, busy summer, I was feeling depleted and far from the Lord's word. Just as those red rocks were completely transformed in His light, I was about to be made new from the blessing of His word.

Sipping my cappuccino, I pondered where to start in the Lord's word. I prayed to the Lord, "What do we do now for our adoption?" and randomly opened up the Bible. His light illuminated these words: "Build up, build up, prepare the road! Remove the obstacles out of the way… For this is what the high and exalted One says." (Isaiah 57:14,15)

In disbelief, I read it again, "Build up, build up, prepare the road! Remove the obstacles out of the way… For this is what the high and lofty One says." I am not sure if I have ever had the Lord answer me that quickly and decisively. I was thrilled. I was shaking in the presence of the Lord, and a smile was pasted onto my face for the entirety of the day.

I did not need to read anymore that day, not the words before or after that scripture. I went to bed with aching cheeks.

Scripture

Isaiah 57:14,15
"Build up, build up, prepare the road! Remove the obstacles out of the way"… For this is what the high and exalted One says.

Thoughts Along the Way

Commit this week to spending time alone with the Lord. Have a cup of coffee with your Father, and quietly read His word. Then jot down what He says to you.

11

MORE THAN A BASKET OF FRUIT

Health, Finances and Support

Images are incredibly powerful. As my adoption to-do list grew, my mind rewound and replayed an image from my visit to the National Gallery of Art almost 12 months earlier. Another of Norman Rockwell's works, *Good Boy (Little Orphan at the Train)*, clarified and ultimately refined my focus and efforts in our adoption process. Rockwell's *Good Boy* painting documents a time in history when orphans were moved from the crowded East Coast cities to the rural Midwest in the latter 1800s. If a feature film were to be made about adoption, this painting could serve as the story's apex. A prospective mother stands on a train platform, about to receive her child into her arms for the first time. She has an anticipatory stance, a longing stare and welcoming arms. At her feet stands a basket of fruit, and that is where my lens focused—on the welcome basket. The Martha Stewart-style arrangements were this mom's visible work of preparation. She made it look so easy. I knew better to accept this painting at face value, though. I understood the planning and preparations that were necessary for a successful adoption, and trust me-it is much more than a basket of fruit.

Yet she looks joyful and absent of the rigors that led up to her big moment. She is solely engaged and fixed on the child she is about to receive, perhaps because she had done *everything* possible to adequately prepare for the arrival of this precious one. I wanted to be like her, so that when I held my child for the first time, he or she was *all* I was focused on because every preparatory detail was complete. My planning needed to be more than a basket of apples or pile of diapers. The "Orphan Train" mom helped me clarify my goal, which was to tackle all the hard stuff upfront.

This painting was the filter through which God's words to "build up" and "prepare the road" became brilliant. The reds were redder, the blues more vibrant, and the issues I needed to attend to were glaring: my health and physical strength, our finances and our parents' cautious concern regarding our adoption decision.

Both Joel and I were almost 40, and I knew full well that a new baby would demand flexibility and an energy level that goes against nature's typical direction. When the Lord said to move the obstacles out of the way, one of those obstacles was my physical health. I imagined myself calming a screaming infant while in the midst of one of my two-day headaches or charging up our flight of stairs fifteen times a day with a twenty-pound baby on my hip. I would need to get healthier and stronger.

My first stop was my wonderful, trusted, compassionate doctor. I walked into his office with a list of concerns, and I walked out with a referral to physical therapy for my headaches, a recommendation for yoga and exercise, and an assurance that he was listening and an ally in my quest to adopt. My two-day-a-week commitment to PT began to strengthen my back and shoulders, improved my posture and reduced my stress headaches.

In addition, yoga and a regular workout routine became part of my adoption preparation. My new exercise regimen brought many unexpected benefits as well. First, it provided me with psychologically tangible evidence of progress. Every time I went to the gym or did physical therapy exercises, I felt our unborn baby was closer to me. It was like limbering up for a downhill run on skis. It may require a bit of painful stretching, but that stretching would be worthwhile when the time came. Second, exercise rejuvenated my optimism. Things were looking up, and the stress I often felt in daily life receded like an ebbtide of worry.

In 1 Corinthians 6:19, the Lord's word reveals this about our health: "Do you not know that your bodies are temples of the Holy Spirit, who is in you, whom you have received from God? You are not your own; you were bought at a price. Therefore honor God with your bodies." I needed to steward my body so that I could honor God with all my life, including fulfilling his calling by staying in shape. This continues even now, when I am struggling to find time to work out and making conscious decisions about what I put on the table. I want to be around when our youngest child graduates from high school and walks down the aisle. The Lord not only called us to adopt her but also to raise her, which will require decades more of good health. The Lord wants us to honor Him and serve Him with our life, and that requires a healthy lifestyle.

The next topic we had to tackle was money. Even writing this makes me cringe. I do not like talking about finances. I would rather do anything else, but ignoring it is impossible. One of Joel's biggest concerns was the financial commitment necessary to see the adoption process through to the end. I shared his concern, but avoided the reality of it.

Our income precisely matched our monthly outlay. We tried to pay the monthly credit card bills to the amount spent, but this was not always possible. Time was against us since the adoption needed to be completed during our current two-year assignment. Missing the deadline would necessitate having to comply with another state's regulations and, to a large extent, starting over. Our estimation was that we needed about $25,000 for the independent adoption we were considering. Joel is good with money, so he had been saving every month for many years. Those funds, however, were specifically earmarked for retirement, college for our children and a future home purchase. Our adoption was not financially planned for in the big picture. But then, who *plans* for adoption? I would venture to say that when most people start saving money in their twenties and thirties (if they saved at all), they did not have an "adoption account" or mutual fund designated "in case of infertility and a calling from God to adopt." The fact is that most of us did not bank on these costs.

One encouraging financial fact when it comes to adoption is that our federal government offers a tax refund/credit to adoptive parents. I was comforted by the fact that we could take advantage of this tax opportunity which, at the time, was about $12,000. I therefore rationalized that our finances only had to accommodate about $13,000.

There were some nuances associated with that refund, however-namely that it was not immediate. (An important note is that the adoption tax credit is a product of legislation, therefore is subject to change. Be sure to look up the current tax law as it relates to adoption, and be an advocate for the adoption tax credit by contacting your elected representatives.) Thus, we were—at least in the short term—faced with paying the full amount. The big numbers were daunting.

Our plan was to first get our current finances in check. We needed to ensure that we were not spending above and beyond our limits in our everyday expenses. I arranged to teach a few more classes to boost our income. Since our route was independent adoption, there was no placement fee as there often is with an agency adoption. The placement fee for an agency adoption can be a large up-front cost. Fortunately, most of the major expenses would come at the completion of the adoption, primarily in the form of attorney costs.

There are a few areas of considerable cost variability to be aware of: the professional status of the lawyer (my advice is look for the *best* American Academy of Adoption Attorney's (AAAA) lawyer in town and pay whatever he or she charges), how much travel will be required, any legal complications of the adoption (if the child is Native American, etc.), and in which state your birth mother resides. As an example of the ways in which costs fluctuate, every state has unique laws that dictate how much financial support an adoptive couple can provide to the birth mother. The law of the state in which the birth mother resides controls how much financial support she can receive from the adoptive parents. Some states prohibit financial support altogether. Other states have no limit. This variability is a significant factor in the financial planning. It will be important to fully understand the regulations of the state in which a potential birth mother resides. There are lists on the Web that cite state specific laws, which provide an easy means of comparison. The state from which we adopted allowed for up to $5,000 in expenses to assist the birth mother. Even though that sounds like a lot of money, it was comforting to know that we could buy our birth mother groceries to feed herself and our child. It was our joy to pay the heating bill so that our baby was not in the womb of a cold mother in the middle of winter. When part of the cost of adoption is to, in effect, help your baby and support your birth mom, that is money you will never regret spending.

In 1 John 3:16-17 it states, "We know what real love is because Jesus gave up his life for us. And so we also ought to give up our lives for our brothers and sisters. If someone has enough money to live well and sees a brother or sister in need but shows no compassion—how can God's love be in that person?" The Lord calls us, when we are able, to help another person in need.

In the final analysis, Joel and I settled on a plan to cover the costs of adoption that was based on a take-it-as-it-comes approach. The fact was that we were not going to be able to pay a $25,000 bill out-of-pocket. Debt was part of our approach.

Planning for the cost of adoption is, for most couples, a major concern in the early stages. Some stop there, never to move beyond the money barrier. My husband, being Mr. Conservative, wanted to know exactly how much the process would cost and precisely how we would pay for it. Although I understood his insistence, I remained firm in my belief that it would somehow work out.

Once again, we leaned on the Lord for a sense of comfort in moving ahead despite not having all the answers, particularly in the area of financial ability. The Lord would not have called us to this place if He did not know we could assume the financial liability of the adoption. While we did not ignore the cost burden, we also did not allow it to be a stopping point for us.

One resource I wished was written when we adopted is *You Can Adopt Without Debt* by Julie Gumm.[1] In that book she has creative and effective suggestions for fundraising, applying for grants and budgeting.

The last critical barrier that needed to be addressed as we prepared the road to adoption was our parents' support of our adoption approach. Once we decided on independent adoption, our opening comment went something like this: "Mom, Dad, we are going to adopt a baby. As you know, it is a calling from the Lord. We are going to advertise for our birth mother on the Web." For some reason we did not receive the round of applause we hoped for.

Joel's parents are faithful followers of the Lord. They understand what a "calling" is, and immediately offered us their support. However, they could not fathom using the Internet to find a baby. Their puzzlement was understandable since, at that point, they barely knew how to use email.

My parents were hung up on their observation that we already had a healthy boy and girl; we were a perfect little family of four. Why dilute the affection we gave to our children by adding another child to an already ideal situation? As we drew closer to starting our home study, I distinctly remember a conversation I had with my Mom. We have a close relationship, and I had shared the ups and downs of the past few years since my calling in Idaho. I kept her in the loop about our decision-making, and had tried to help her understand our relentless drive to adopt. However, my patience with her negativity had worn out. In so many words I said, "This ship is going to sail with or without your approval." I wanted her to be part of this journey, but I also knew I needed to surround myself with people who were going to encourage me and help me through the year. After that conversation, her Negative Nelly talk turned to Positive Polly.

Gradually, our parents came to realize that no amount of doubt on their part was going to lessen our determination. Once on board, they threw in their full weight behind us. Their doubting turned to "What can we do to help?"

You may find that being transparent in your plan as it progresses is helpful to gaining others' support. But there may also come a time when the conversation changes from "What do you think?" to "This is going to happen, whether you agree with it or not."

The Lord says in 2 Corinthians 6:6-8: "We serve God whether people honor us or despise us, whether they slander us or praise us." His will for our lives is supreme. Your effort to adopt cannot be thwarted by anyone. It may be that those who communicate the most doubt are the closest members of your family, and this likely happens because they care most about you and are protective of your well-being. It will also be those same people who, when they see the Lord's plan come to fruition, will be the most pleased to hold this precious child.

Paul's instructions to the Church in Corinth, found in 1 Corinthians 3:6-10, speaks to preparation.

> "I planted the seed, Apollos watered it, but God has been making it grow. So neither the one who plants nor the one who waters is anything, but only God, who makes things grow. The one who plants and the one who waters have one purpose, and they will each be rewarded according to their own labor. For we are co-workers in God's service."

We are God's co-workers in adoption-the ones pedaling. It is critical to identify obstacles unique to your circumstance and "build up" so that your adoption can proceed on a clear path. Before long you, too, will hear the train whistle blow and find yourself on a platform of God's grace, extending your arms to welcome a child chosen for you.

Scripture

1 Corinthians 6:19-20
Do you not know that your bodies are temples of the Holy Spirit, who is in you, whom you have received from God? You are not your own; you were bought at a price. Therefore honor God with your bodies.

1 John 3:16-17 (NLT)
We know what real love is because Jesus gave up his life for us. And so we also ought to give up our lives for our brothers and sisters. If someone has enough money to live well and sees a brother or sister in need but shows no compassion—how can God's love be in that person?

2 Corinthians 6:8 (NLT)
We serve God whether people honor us or despise us, whether they slander us or praise us.

1 Corinthians 3:6-9
I planted the seed, Apollos watered it, but God has been making it grow. So neither the one who plants nor the one who waters is anything, but only God, who makes things grow. The one who plants and the one who waters have one purpose, and they will each be rewarded according to their own labor. For we are co-workers in God's service.

Thoughts Along the Way

Jot down the obstacles you see that may impede your adoption. Then consider a few areas of focus that would allow you to "build-up" in preparation for your adoption.

Do you have a good doctor? Someone you trust and who is responsive to you? I've noticed that many of my close friends do not seek out a *good* doctor. Once your child is in your arms, your needs will become secondary. Having a good doctor in place will be a source of solace if you become sick or have health issues. Spend the time now to find a trusted partner in your health.

12

MARTHA MODE

The Home Study

From train tracks to vacuum tracks, the adoption process was in full swing as we started our home study. I received the home study checklist from the social worker we hired and charged full steam ahead.

First on the list: the medical exam. Our appointment day came, and I reminded Joel that morning to be home by noon for the checkup. This included a blood draw, vitals, urine check and a quick physical. Still in uniform, Joel literally ran to his car from the courtroom on his lunch break to meet the traveling nurse. Navigating the 45 minutes in Washington D.C. traffic to make it home on time, Joel was met at our front door with a blood pressure cuff and a cup to pee in. Needless to say, the nurse had to coach him through some breathing techniques to get his blood pressure to an acceptable level. The home study is all of these things: uncomfortable, chaotic, frustrating and stressful. In a counter-intuitive way, however, it is the easiest and most clear-cut task in the entire process. Allow me to explain.

Control feels good. It is part of human nature for us to desire, seek and feel comforted by a sense of control in our lives. As a therapist, I've counseled people who grasp at control through food, relationships, or rigid routines. Personally, I seek control through a microfiber cloth and a bottle of Pledge. If I am stressed and feeling like life is getting out of my tight grip, I dust. My house has never looked as good as it did when we were adopting.

Adoption is a tough road because, to a large extent, the final outcome is out of your control. Remember the whole back seat, tandem bike thing? However, there are some bright spots of perceived control, and the home study is one of them. The term home study does not imply homework in the same way it is doled out by a high school teacher. It is a study and, ultimately, a report that is filed with the court that addresses every conceivable dimension of the adoptive parents' personal circumstances. What is required of the adoptive parents comes in the form of a checklist. The straight forward, two-page form with check boxes was a glorious, bright spot in the thick FPA binder.

My goal was to quickly and efficiently get the home study completed so that we could start advertising for a birth mom. This was a necessary step before advertising because many adoption websites require a home study in order to post a profile. Since we were not connected with an agency, we were able to select and hire our social worker for the home study. Another golden point in favor of independent adoption: choice!

Having attended the FPA seminar that featured several speakers with an expertise in the key steps for independent adoption, I felt confident in the qualities I was seeking in a home study social worker. Wise words were imprinted that day: "The only way to flunk a home study (the only official evaluative piece in adoption) is to have a criminal history or pick a fight with your social worker." A no-drama, matter-of-fact, check-the-box social worker is what we sought. Home study social workers have probably seen a million miles of vacuum tracks. Sorting out the criminals is their mission, not ranking you or comparing you to other qualified adoptive couples. The key is to find a proficient social worker who will follow up with phone calls and keep the process running smoothly so that you get in and out of the home study quickly with an approval to adopt. That social worker's approval will eventually land on a judge's desk, and will be the basis for his or her determination of your ability to care for a child.

If you are connected with an agency, you may have less of a choice when it comes to who completes your home study. If, for some reason, you don't get along with the social worker you are assigned, consult the director of the agency and ask for a different home study professional. Remember, you are still the consumer in this process. Money has been paid, and you deserve to have services that meet your needs.

Once you begin the home study process, the hoop-jumping begins! Fingerprinting and criminal clearances are part of the checklist. I found it interesting that the hours of operation for the fingerprint facility are often 9-5 Monday through Friday; they take a 2-hour break for lunch, are closed the second Monday of the month and have half-days every third Friday. While taking off work wasn't an issue for me, it became frustrating for Joel to find times that coordinated with the convoluted state agency hours of operation.

There is a laundry list of requirements: collecting records, calculating finances, seeking references, documenting personal and family histories, discussing the finer points of carbon monoxide detectors with the local fire marshal, undergoing a home check, and completing medical exams to validate your (and your other children's) health. There are minor state-to-state variations for home study requirements. Some parents become concerned that the nursery and all baby proofing must be complete at the time of the home study. Most social workers I have worked with do not include this as part of the home study requirements. Social workers are more interested in whether there is generally adequate physical space in the home for a child.

The financial calculations are done by way of a financial statement that lays out your income, debt and investments. Again, this is not to prove that you can cover the cost of a $25,000 adoption out-of-pocket; it is simply to demonstrate that you are financially responsible and can afford to care for a child.

The personal interview is a component of the home study that may or may not be difficult, depending on how much personal baggage you currently have or have dealt with in your life. Joel had a model childhood, so his personal interview was about 39 seconds long. Mine, on the other hand, was a bit lengthier. Both my parents are loving, and I truly had a fabulous childhood, but their divorce was something that the social worker wanted to touch upon. The bottom line for the personal interview is that hard questions might be asked. Just be ready to face them head on, and demonstrate resolution to any difficult chapters in your life. Your history does not have to be perfect, the court simply wants to know that you are mentally sound and have unloaded any baggage that may have been heaped upon you as a child.

The question to watch out for is, "What are your expectations for this child?" This is, in my opinion, the only question that might throw you for a loop. Social workers like to ensure that you understand that your adopted child is unique, with strengths and capabilities that might not neatly fit into your conceptualization of who they will be or become. You may be tempted to answer with something to the effect of, "We will provide this baby with every affordance to ensure that his academic surroundings are rich. It will be important that he go to college and pursue a professional job so that he will never be a victim of poverty." That's the wrong answer. It sounds good, but it's the wrong answer. Let's try again.

"We understand that this child will have unique strengths and abilities. Our goal is to provide this child with the love and nurturing that will allow him to reach his full potential—whatever that may be."

Social history: check. Home inspection: check. Marriage license: check. Criminal background history: check. I had checked off nearly every box. We finally made it to the family interview with the social worker. Nothing was going to jump out and surprise me so close to the end, right? Well…

On the way to the social worker's office, we talked to the kids about being honest, but also clearly stated that this was not the time to be silly. We walked into the small office, took our seats on the couch and nervously waited for the firing squad of questions. Kelsey was up first; she breezed through with social prowess. Next, it was Alex's turn. He was then seven years old. The social worker asked, "What do you think about having a baby sister or brother?" His response was, "I am really excited. I can teach the baby how to spit." And there went my control right out the window.

As you check the boxes and leave frantic vacuum tracks on your carpet in anticipation of the home visit, it's important that you not morph into Martha. You know Martha, right? Here is a snapshot of her story:

> As Jesus and his disciples were on their way, he came to a village where a woman named Martha opened her home to him. She had a sister called Mary, who sat at the Lord's feet listening to what he said. But Martha was distracted by all the preparations that had to be made. She came to him and asked, "Lord, don't

> you care that my sister has left me to do the work by myself? Tell her to help me!"
>
> "Martha, Martha," the Lord answered, "you are worried and upset about many things, but few things are needed—or indeed only one. Mary has chosen what is better, and it will not be taken away from her." Luke 10:38-42

The Lord's words may need repeating. "You are worried and upset about many things, but few things are needed—or indeed only one."

The details of the home study can easily push you into Martha-mode and cause you to lose sight of the big picture. Even if there are hiccups along the way, His plan is more powerful than a financial statement with a bit of red ink on it or a social history with a few black marks.

The key is to model after Mary. Because what you *will not* find on the home study checklist is:

- Sit at His feet and listen to the Lord
- Pray
- Read His word

Check those boxes first, then move on to the rest and I assure you that the final report will glowingly recommend you as fantastic parents!

Scripture

Luke 10:41-42
"Martha, Martha," the Lord answered, "you are worried and upset about many things, but few things are needed—or indeed only one."

Thoughts Along the Way

Are you Mary or Martha? What makes you so?

Having insight into who you are is the first step in making changes toward who you want to be more like.

13

FIJI WATER AND THE PENNYSAVER

Creating Your Profile

As Joel and I sat in our lawyer's posh outer office, high above the bustling men and women in suits and honking horns on the downtown D.C. city streets, we sank into deep leather chairs and sipped Fiji bottled water. Assuaging our adoption fears were Mr. McDermott's many degrees hanging on the walls as well as the awards he received as the past President of the American Academy of Adoption Attorneys standing on the cherry wood shelf. Mark might as well have been Santa Claus, and his gift to us was his sound adoption advice.

"His eyes—how they twinkled! His dimples, how merry! His cheeks were like roses, his nose like a cherry!" Just as the night before Christmas brings an overwhelming sense of joy and anticipation, Joel and I looked up with hopeful eyes to a man delivering us a wrapped present. We hung on every word. And then, with the "wink of his eye and a twist of his head," he unexpectedly slipped a piece of coal in our stocking by way of the word "advertising." (Please be aware that states vary widely on laws regarding advertising and the role of the lawyer in independent adoption. There are some states that allow the lawyer to act as a facilitator and connect birth moms to prospective birth parents, but most do not. It is critical to consult an attorney to learn the laws of the state in which you reside).

Was he serious? We had to advertise for our baby? Not only that, we were advised *not* to place a full-color ad in the *New York Times* but instead to take out a simple 2-inch by 2-inch ad in the Pennysaver. Our attorney handed me a yellowed copy of the Pennysaver; I set down my bottle of water and began to browse the adoption ads. Mark pointed to the small black-and-white boxes and began differentiating between the effective ads and the "duds."

Somehow, I did not like the flavor of his advice—that my child might be found through the Pennysaver. I thought back to my college days when I was looking for a cheap dresser for my college dorm room; I believe the Pennysaver was the throw-away paper I picked up outside the Circle K. Here it was, a "Johnnie Walker Red" moment—the realization that if we were going to pursue independent adoption, our child may come to be ours through the Pennysaver. That piece of information took a while to sink in.

In addition to the Pennysaver, Mark also advised that we post our profile on several adoption websites aimed at matching prospective adoptive parents with pregnant women considering adoption. These companies charge a fee for couples to post a profile and they, in turn, maximize your online profile exposure. Initially, this sounded like a breeding ground for scams to me. In time, it came to be the means by which we connected with our birth mom. (NOTE: The effectiveness of these profiling sites is constantly in flux. Thus, it is critical to reach out to others who are currently adopting to assess which sites are most effective.)

My perspective began to change, however, the more I understood about a birth mother's circumstance. My conception of a birth mother was based solely on the movie "Juno." The picture I constructed in my head of a birth mom involved a woman who had mistakenly gotten pregnant, wanted to pursue a college education and realized that having a child at this point in her life would hinder her ultimate goal of becoming a pediatrician. I was a bit off the mark. Mark brought me back to reality and shared that most birth mothers find themselves in a place of desperation—financially, relationally and emotionally when they decide to place their child for adoption.

It is the free Pennysaver next to the metro station that a birth mom randomly picks up in the early morning darkness as she boards the train on her way to her minimum wage job. The words "Let's help each other" leap off the page, and she jots down a phone number on her hand. Or, it may be the birth mother who uses the local library to access the Internet and sees a pop-up ad. Through the screen stares a loving, secure couple who offer a bright light of hope for her unborn child, and she clicks the link and writes a brief email sharing her situation. This is how it happens.

Mark's advice was to *cast as wide a net as possible.* These were the steps we took to get the word out:

- We made a Facebook page just for our adoption quest and asked everyone we knew to "Like" and "Share" it.
- We described our desire to adopt in our Christmas letter and included business cards with our picture and Facebook page for our friends and family to distribute, post and share.
- We made postcard fliers to post in public community spaces (Starbucks, the local pool, the college where I taught, etc.).

- We distributed business cards at every restaurant, left them in empty grocery carts, and handed them out to people we met standing in lines, etc.
- We advertised in the Pennysaver and the local community college newspaper.
- We created a family profile and advertised through Parent Profiles on the Web.

If we were adopting now, we would also take these advertising steps:

- We would use YouTube to post a family video.
- We would include Instagram for social media advertising.
- We would create our own website.
- We would seek out "waiting family" lists and pay the nominal fees to have our profile be shown to potential birth moms-without paying the super high "placement fees" that traditional agencies charge. Select AAAA lawyers and some agencies offer this service- check out the one at MomentumAdoptions.com

If the above suggestions for advertising makes the privacy red flag fly high in your conscience, you are not alone in that initial response. It is a hurdle that one must come to terms with on the independent adoption route. The fact is, if you are going to have a successful *independent* adoption, you will need to forgo some degree of privacy to get your profile seen by birth mothers.

Families for Private Adoption (FPA) has incredible workshops that are offered both face-to-face and online that thoroughly explain advertising options, among other critical independent adoption information. Even if you can not attend one of their workshops, it is worth it to purchase the workbook, which can be ordered from their website www.FFPA.org.

Below is the postcard flier I created:

Below is the advertisement we used in the Pennysaver:

All these efforts took a considerable amount of time, but the most labor intensive was creating our family profile, sometimes called a "Dear Birth Mom" letter. Whether you choose an independent adoption or an agency adoption, most prospective adoptive parents come to the place of sitting down at the computer and compressing their entire life into a two page document. Much like a resume, it is a shaping of words to mold your family in the best light.

I read many profiles prior to writing ours. I wanted to get a sense of what other couples were sharing and how they presented that information. I also labored over which pictures to include or omit. If there is one overriding principle when describing a family's character, it is that of defining a value system that provides a loving, secure environment for a child yet to be born. Having spent many hours belaboring the most minuscule points, I had a draft that I shared with another couple in our FPA group. She made some helpful suggestions, and then we posted. Another good idea might be to seek feedback on the profile from a few twenty-something-year-old women, since that is your target audience. If you are seeking a professional to ensure your profile is going to grab a birth mom's attention, a top-notch adoption profiler is Purl Adoption Advisory. They are the masters at creating stand-out family profiles.

Here is the crux of the situation: you simply don't know what is going to catch the eye of your birth mom. Maybe it's the fact that you have brown hair, or grew up in Connecticut, or maybe it's that your husband looks like her favorite uncle. One adoptive mother shared with me that the birth mom initially chose their profile because they had a shared favorite candy-Reece's Pieces. You just cannot predict. Be honest, and paint as accurate a picture of your life as you can. Less text, more pictures. Try to include pictures of you being active or engaging with children (neighbor kids or nieces or nephews).

When we met with our birthparents for the first time, we began sharing details of our lives. One vital piece of information revealed by our birthparents was that they were Green Bay Packer fans. Wow, I was glad we didn't advertise our affinity for the Pittsburgh Steelers; that may have changed the course of history!

My final piece of advice is, do not post any potentially divisive information, such as your political views and, yes, your favorite sports team. Once you have created your profile, step back and take a look at it. One certainty is this: you are the perfect family for your child. *You* are not perfect, of course, but you are the ideal family for your child. Know that a birth mother will look at your profile and chose you to be her child's parent(s).

For most going public with personal information is terrifying, mostly for fear of inviting scammers into the family fold. Once we started the search for our baby, my guard was high for both financial and emotional scams. However, my trepidation was temporary. We became savvy consumers and were quick to pick up red flags. When we made decisions to follow up with birth moms, we were confident that they had their child's best interest at heart. There are several helpful online forums to identify scams where prospective adoptive parents report suspicious emails and texts from persons posing as expectant mothers. You may want to search Facebook groups that are tracking some of these potential scams (*Putting an End to Adoption Scams*, etc.). Another resource is a closed forum that is offered through membership in FPA. The FPA forum had many independent adoption couples posting their experiences and reporting potential scams when they found them. It really kept our finger on the pulse with regard to potential scam artists. In all, we encountered only two "phishing" emails that were not legitimate.

A few more points of advice that were helpful when we began advertising:

- Get a toll-free number. There are many companies that offer this service for free.
- Create a separate adoption email address-do not include your last name.

- Purchase a separate adoption phone-make sure that phone has texting capability.

Even though we could have used my cell phone to accept calls, we followed Mark's advice and bought an "adoption only" phone, and I am very glad we did. It helped us compartmentalize the adoption. The part-time job of adoption can be all-consuming if you allow it. Small efforts such as having a separate phone helped to keep a line drawn in the sand between our daily lives and our adoption quest. Another positive aspect about the adoption phone was that when it rang, all hands were on deck. Our kids knew to be quiet, I knew to pick up no matter what was going on and Joel knew to get into adoption mode if he had the phone.

One afternoon, Alex had a friend over for a playdate. They were playing a game downstairs when the adoption phone rang in the adjacent room. Alex yelled up to me, as I was folding laundry. "The adoption phone is ringing," he hollered. I bolted downstairs, dashed through the living room, stumbled over a Nerf gun, and quickly answered. Alex's friend returned home that afternoon and shared with his mom, "...their adoption phone rang; I didn't know Mrs. England could run *that* fast."

The toll-free number allows a prospective birth mom, many of whom are without the financial resources necessary to own a cell phone, to call you. The bottom line is that if you can eliminate a barrier to communication, it is beneficial to do so. It also makes sense to keep a separate email for any and all adoption communication. This keeps your private email account confidential and provides for a distinct place for all adoption-related communication. You do not want a birth mother's email getting buried in your everyday, overloaded inbox!

Our birthparents had no Internet access, so they used the public library's free web access. As they were looking at various websites about pregnancy and adoption, our profile popped up. In the short time they were at the library, they looked at two profiles. Ours was one of them. That was it! The timing of that pop-up advertisement was all in the Lord's hands.

The nature of the Internet and social media is ever-changing. What worked last year, might not be an effective strategy this year. One way to keep current on effective search strategies is to consult with a professional (try Momentum Adoptions 30 minute consultation to get up-to-date search strategy information).

As for your "Dear Birth Mom" letter, you can debate whether or not to use the picture of you smiling at your wedding or the one of you and your niece splashing in the ocean on your vacation in Florida, but remember that God will have a hand in your birth mom choosing you. It won't be luck. In the end, the Lord will connect you and your birth mom.

The Lord says in Jeremiah 29:13: "You will seek me and find me when you seek me with all your heart." The Lord's encouragement is that if you seek, you *will* find. The key is seeking with all your heart. It is easy when you are in advertising mode to become all about your visibility to the birth mom. How many hits did our page get? Did we post that postcard in the most visible spot on the community bulletin board? What did our Google Analytics report spit out as the most trafficked advertisement? One way to fight against that tendency and keep your heart in the right place is to pray. Pray when you post! My prayer sounded something like this: "Lord, I know you have our baby in mind. Help me to trust in your plan fully. Thank you for bringing me to this point, and help to prepare me for meeting our birth mom in the coming months."

Rest assured that the Lord is working from up above and has a better vantage point than you for what needs to happen.

Scripture

Jeremiah 29:13
You will seek me and find me when you seek me with all your heart

Thoughts Along the Way

Whether you chose independent or agency adoption, there will be a time when you will have to create a profile to share your life with a prospective birth mother. If you could describe yourself (and then your spouse or partner) in three words, what would they be? Consider using pictures that best depict these three qualities.

Put in the time to make your profile/advertisements great. Pray when you post, and then leave the rest to the Lord.

14

THE PLACES YOU'LL GO

Choosing a Birth Mom in Accordance with God's Will

Joel was on adoption phone duty when he received a call from an 18- year-old who was 5 months pregnant. She had seen our advertisement in the Pennysaver and nervously shared that she and her fiancé could not take care of a baby since neither of them had a job. Because transportation was an issue, we agreed that we would meet in a location close to their home. Joel and I anxiously waited outside a diner called China Palace, leaning against barred windows and double-checking to make sure the car was locked. One small detail Joel had omitted was the importance of seeking out identifying factors to help us recognize the couple. Across the parking lot we spotted a Hispanic male and a young African American woman with a small baby bump. Hoping this was the couple from the Pennysaver, we introduced ourselves. I tried to appear relaxed, but my sweaty palms may have revealed my true state of emotion.

I had memorized a list of pertinent questions to ask in our initial meeting, but my preparation faded in the excitement of the moment. I reached into my Psychology 101 bag of teaching lectures and pulled out one from Carl Rogers, a famous psychologist. He emphasized three characteristics that are necessary for productive human interaction: warmth, empathy and genuineness (collectively referred to as WEG). The challenge would be to utilize all the WEG I could muster, yet still interject the critical questions I knew were important to our decision.

I began by asking about the couple's personal story, which they eagerly described. Shortly after sitting down with our egg roll and hot tea, however, it became apparent that the expectant father was not completely on board with adoption; in fact, he had not stepped even one foot on deck. After a few bites of mildly warm fried rice and an initial comment about adoption, he half choked and sputtered, "I thought you were joking when you said we were meeting them to talk about adoption." This begged the question, "Well, *why* did you think you were meeting?" But at this point I could only understand half of what they were saying because they were arguing in Spanish, so I let my thought remain unspoken. Making this meeting a bit more comedic was Joel's poker face. After fifteen years of marriage, I could tell he was thinking, *"Really? This is the path to our child?"* Our birth mother meet-and-greet morphed into a couple's therapy session, with me mediating conflict over an unplanned pregnancy.

Other than the obvious fact that the expectant father was caught off guard by his fiancé's intentions, the conversation revealed major cultural barriers to adoption. He was palms-up distressed when imagining his family's reaction to an adoption decision. That day, we learned how critical cultural norms are in adoption. A complex, sticky web of culture and family values can either be a safety net for a successful adoption or a menacing trap for failure. Thus, it is wise to thoroughly explore these areas before choosing a birth mother.

By the end of the meeting, it was clear that this couple was not on the same page. Our departing comment was, "If you decide that adoption is right for you, please give us a call." We had a hunch that this couple would never again dial our phone number.

The path to our birth family was not a straight line. There were sharp corners, potholes that caused us to swerve and disappointing dead-ends. We learned to balance our instincts with a rational evaluation of each contact.

As humans we crave choice. The thought of having some choice in selecting our birth mom and ultimately our child was wildly attractive. Yet that choice brings with it difficult decision-making. This became evident when we were faced with a checklist on our adoption profile application titled, *What You are Open To*. This checklist included items like: maternal drug exposure, bi-racial, African American, Hispanic, boy, girl, under 2 years old, older than 2 years old, major genetic abnormality, unknown birth father, etc. At this point we were forced to have a tough conversation.

The foundation of our adoption was that we would adopt one of His children, but weren't they all His? How could we check one box and not another? This was an emotional push and pull on our hearts. Joel and I were able to navigate this hurdle by framing it in a strengths-based and faith-based window. We had to look at our God-given gifts, life experiences, our environment, and our current family situation to assess our unique strengths that would provide the optimal goodness-of-fit for this child in our family. One way to conceptualize this process is more of *discernment in matching* than of checking or not checking boxes. God has blessed each of us with unique gifts and talents. These are the strengths that He has purposefully provided so that His will may be done on this earth.

Once we identified our strengths and those variables that we thought would provide the best fit and best chance for a successful adoption, we completed the checklist and also put together a list of pointed questions to ask a potential birth mom. Since I knew I would be nervous when a birth mom called, I taped (I literally minimized the font and Scotch-taped) the following questions to my adoption phone:

- *I'm so glad you called. Do you mind me asking what has brought you to have an interest in adoption? I'd love to hear your story.
- *How are you feeling? Have you had any complications? Is this your first pregnancy?
- *What state do you live in?
- *Have you seen a doctor yet? Do you know the due date?
- *Who else supports you in this adoption plan?
- *What relationship do you have with the father of the baby?
- *Does your family and birth father's family know about the pregnancy? What do they think of a possible adoption?
- *What support system do you have to help you through this?
- *What are you looking for in an adoption plan?
- *Why adoption?
- Tell me about yourself.
- If you did have the baby, how would you support yourself?

- How old are you?
- Are you still in school?
- Have you had any counseling with regard to your decision?
- What did you like about our profile?
- Are you working?
- Have you smoked, drank or done drugs while pregnant?

*The questions with an asterisk by them are the ones that were critical to us when making a decision about whether or not to travel for a face-to-face meeting.

It is likely that most questions will be answered in the course of a natural conversation, which is far preferable to a structured list of topics. But it is good to know which questions *need* to be answered so that they can be addressed if, by the end of the conversation, you did not touch on them.

One commonality we found is that women considering adoption are in crisis. Their situation is most often one of deprivation of some sort, perhaps a loss of relationship or simply being too young to handle the responsibility of a child. You will most likely also hear stories of drug addiction and financial desperation.

As you decide on the "deal breakers" for your adoption, keep in mind that having too many can create limits. Set your boundaries knowing that the fourth year Harvard student who had a one-night stand, is completely sober, a health nut, and comes from an intact loving family is not going to be the norm. It's important to have flexibility within predefined boundaries that are wide enough to accommodate most circumstances.

Dr. Seuss's book, *Oh the Places You'll Go*, quite accurately portrays the journey of an adoptive parent:

"You will come to a place where the streets are not marked.
Some windows are lighted. But mostly they're darked.
A place you could sprain both your elbow and chin!
Do you dare to stay out? Do you dare to go in?
How much can you lose? How much can you win?

And IF you go in, should you turn left or right…
or right-and-three-quarters? Or, maybe, not quite?
Or go around back and sneak in from behind?
Simple it's not, I'm afraid you will find,
for a mind-maker-upper to make up his mind.

You can get so confused
that you'll start in to race
down long wiggled roads at a break-necking pace
and grind on for miles across weirdish wild space,
headed, I fear, toward a most useless place.
The Waiting Place…

…for people just waiting.
And will you succeed?
Yes! You will, indeed!"[1]

Do you hear his optimism and positivity? It is the same resolute statement our attorney made at the start of our adoption: "You *will* adopt as long as you hang in there long enough." And it is the Lord's promise also. We see that in Jeremiah 29:11: "For I know the plans I have for you," declares the LORD, "plans to prosper you and not to harm you, plans to give you hope and a future." You are here for a reason, put in this exact place purposefully by our Lord and Savior. Your search for a birth mother is not about finding a needle in a haystack, or random luck or happenstance. As Beth Moore, the great Bible teacher, reminds us, "The Lord said your name before he said, "Let there be Light.""[2] The birth mother you are seeking has already been found. Like you, she is waiting. It is just a matter of connecting.

The Lord has powerful words for us in this time of seeking, and they center upon prayer. When you are searching for a birth mom, it's your job to seek and ultimately choose, but also to discern God's will for your life and the life of your child.

I want to pause on the word "discern." Its definition is "perception in the absence of judgment with a view to obtaining spiritual direction and understanding."[3] Let's rewind and go back over that in slow motion. "Perception...with a view to obtain spiritual direction and understanding." Our choices must be made from a place where our viewpoint is focused on God's will. That is a lofty task that will require much consultation with God. Thus, prayer is a necessity!

In Proverbs 2:1-5, God's word advises us: "Accept my words and store up my commands within you, turning your ear to wisdom and applying your heart to understanding - indeed, if you call out for insight and cry aloud for understanding, and if you look for it as for silver and search for it as for hidden treasure, then you will understand the fear of the LORD and find the knowledge of God." During this decision-making period, you are on a search for God's direction as if it were silver or gold. Prayer is what you need most right now. Go to Him and ask for His counsel and guidance.

Scripture

Jeremiah 29:11
For I know the plans I have for you," declares the LORD, "plans to prosper you and not to harm you, plans to give you hope and a future. "

Proverbs 2:1-5
Accept my words and store up my commands within you, turning your ear to wisdom and applying your heart to understanding-indeed, if you call out for insight and cry aloud for understanding, and if you look for it as for silver and search

for it as for hidden treasure, then you will understand the fear of the LORD and find the knowledge of God.

Thoughts Along the Way

As you begin to discern regarding a birth mom, write down your first impressions of birth mother and birth father encounters. I am more than glad I took the time to jot down my thoughts and record our conversations in pen. I read back and am reminded of God's presence in every word spoken.

15

VALLEYS RISE AND MOUNTAINS CRUMBLE

Meeting Your Birth Mom

I stuffed towels into the kids' pool bag, threw in a few dollars for the Naval Academy pool's entrance fee and added two fruit roll-ups in anticipation of swim-hungry kids needing to make it until lunch. Joel, the kids and I headed out the door into summer sunshine on a Saturday dedicated to family fun. Closing the car door, I checked my purse to make sure the adoption phone was on and the ringer was set to high. My ears were perked like a highly anxious cat, waiting for the sound of the ringtone.

As we pulled out of the driveway, Joel and I were in high-alert mode, involved in several ongoing conversations with potential birth mothers. Two days prior, we received an email from an expectant mother. It read, "Hi, I am 2 months pregnant. I have three other children who are four years old, two years old, 7 months old. I am doing adoption and have to find a family. Please call me whenever. Thank you very much." My heart did a cautious leap. I replied to her email immediately and, of course, I called her first thing in the morning. The phone rang, but there was no answer. My mind conjured up worst case scenarios. Maybe it was a scam. Maybe they already chose a different couple. I had to deliberately pull my attention to other things in order to stay sane. We received a reply email the next day. Again, I promptly responded.

So here we were on the morning of our family-fun pool day, and I wanted to try calling once again. With a stern, "Shhhh" directed toward the backseat, I shared with the kids that I was making an important call. They knew never to trifle with the adoption phone and, in a rare moment of obedience, hushed their activity. One ring, two rings, and a deep voice answered. Every word out of my mouth was weighted. "Hello, I am calling to speak with Caroline." I tried to conceal my emotion. I assumed it was Michael, whom Caroline had described in her email. From her communication, it sounded as though he was supportive of the adoption plan, but I did not want to specifically state why I was calling. Therefore, I did not expand upon the reason for my call and instead, simply asked if Caroline could call me back. End of call. Bummer. My stomach sunk.

As we continued on to the Naval Academy pool and crossed over the Severn River, my eyes were glued to the serene scene. Leisurely couples were sailing, children were playing on the bank of the river and folks were lowering their crab baskets from the pier into the rippling water. Oh how I wanted to be a part of their peaceful, summer moment. But my body was so tight that it would take a lot of summer days at the pool and strolls on the Annapolis harbor to undo the adoption anxiety, which was growing exponentially.

Just as we entered into the pool's parking lot, the adoption phone rang. My body shot a healthy dose of adrenaline, and I hopefully answered. "Hello."

It was Caroline returning my call. In response to my gestures, the kids and Joel silently shuffled out of the car, and I remained. Windows down, I purposefully kept my seatbelt fastened. Maybe I remained buckled in order to feel safety in a moment riddled with risk, or maybe I was so inflated with excitement that I supposed I might float up into the clear blue sky.

I had many questions that I wanted to ask, but the social worker in me knew that listening had to be my top priority. I genuinely wanted to hear her story. I hung on every word she shared and took a few notes to ensure that I remembered to tell Joel the details of our conversation. In my head, I had rehearsed what I might say to a birth mom many times. Should I share that our desire to adopt stems from a calling from the Lord? Or will she just think I am some sort of zealous Christian nut case? Our conversation revealed that Caroline held very strong views on abortion. She also had solid Christian beliefs rooted in the faithful examples of her grandparents and mother. I shared honestly, and we connected on the deepest level possible. It was agreed that this was a plan higher than both of our own doings.

From the start, Caroline graciously, boldly, and genuinely told us, "I want this child to be a gift to your family." Can you imagine the strength of a young woman—one who has inconceivable pressures in her life—having the perspective to believe and say that? After about some thirty plus minutes of intense conversation, we said goodbye. Tears rolling down my face, all I could do was incessantly repeat the words, "Thank you" as I prayed to the Lord. Regaining my composure, I tossed the keys and adoption phone in my purse, jumped onto my shaky legs and, full of anticipation, hurried to tell Joel the good news.

We felt completely positive about our connection with Caroline, but what was our next step? Joel suggested we call Mark for advice. When we first met with Mark, he predicted that there would be times that we would need to act more quickly than felt comfortable. This was one of those times. He sternly barked, "Green light…go." I asked him for clarification.

"Go," as in "Go meet with Caroline and Michael?" Mark was as steadfast as could be in his advice.

"Yes. And ASAP."

This took both Joel and me by surprise. Really? After one phone conversation with a potential birth mother, the wisest, most experienced adoption lawyer in the land was advising a trip to Wisconsin ASAP. While we were hesitant to invest such money and time into a one-call relationship, we trusted Mark and followed his lead. We booked the trip.

Just two weeks had elapsed between our first email contact and our projected trip to Wisconsin. Joel and I touched down in Milwaukee and rolled out of the rental car garage for the two-hour drive through rural Wisconsin. I was calm as a cucumber on the flight—and even in the car—with Joel at the wheel. Making good time, we had a few hours to spare and stopped at an outlet mall, where we purchased two outfits, one for a baby boy and one for a baby girl. With some trepidation I bought the sweet infant clothes. I did not want to presuppose the outcome of our meeting with Caroline but, in my heart, I felt confident that this was going to be our baby, that this was the Lord's will.

Back on the highway, just a few exits from our destination, my nerves began to shudder. Questions of doubt started to flood my conscience as Joel navigated through the quaint Wisconsin town. "What if they don't show for our meeting? Are we crazy for flying halfway across the country to meet strangers we met on the Internet?" It sure sounded crazy!

We checked into a Main Street hotel, and I called Caroline to confirm we were still on track for our afternoon meeting. Yes, everything was going according to plan. Deep breath.

What should I wear? Jeans or leggings, a soft colored sweater or a bright red top so she won't miss me? Maybe I should just wear a fluorescent sweatshirt that reads, "Here to Adopt!" In all reality, what I wore did not matter, it was what we said and whether a genuine connection would be made.

Just a few hours later, with sweaty hands and racing hearts, we waited in the hotel lobby. Each time the automatic double doors opened, I jumped. I stood with a small bag containing Playdough and other kid-friendly activities that Kelsey and Alex had lovingly collected to help us connect with her little ones. In this moment of waiting I didn't know if we were just two fools following the advice of an over-zealous adoption attorney or if we were about to have a life-changing encounter.

Just when I thought I could not bear another second, we set eyes on sweet Caroline, a towering Michael and their three adorable children. As we settled into a conversation, one of the first statements I made was, "We've been waiting so long for this very moment, and I am full of nerves right now." Our birth mother let out a burst of nervous laughter, "us too." Acknowledging that we were all tense helped calm the waters.

Caroline and Michael were so attentive and loving toward their children. We could see right away that they were good parents. In between dipping toes in the indoor hotel pool and crafting Playdough pancakes in an empty conference room, we started creating a bond that would end up being lifelong.

An unexpected blessing sealed our confidence in this match. Caroline invited her mother, Julia, to also meet with us that day. Julia came later that evening, bearing family photo albums. We all sat on the floor in the lobby turning pages and soaking in the pictures of our birth mom's life. In Julia's tears, I saw a commitment to her daughter and this unborn child. She was in full agreement with the plan for adoption.

In Isaiah 40:3, we find these words: "In the wilderness prepare the way for the LORD; make straight in the desert highway for our God. Every valley shall be raised up, every mountain and hill made low; the rough ground shall become level, the rugged places a plain. And the glory of the LORD will be revealed, and all people will see it together. For the mouth of the LORD has spoken."

You, my friend, over the past months and years have been doing just this in your adoption preparation. You have removed obstacles and worked hard to ensure a clear highway for the Lord's will in your life through adoption. In God's perfect timing, you will see the glory of the Lord in your sweet child's eyes.

From the moment we posted our profile online, I asked the Lord to make our birth mother stand out. There was no doubt I was committed to "pedaling" and preparing a way for the Lord's plan, but I needed Him to make it clear whom we could trust. I prayed that he would make His will for us crystal clear. This He did! I watched the valleys rise in Caroline's smile, the mountains crumble at Michael's calmness and the rugged plains made smooth by Julia's steadfast support. The path we had traveled for so long became level, and we felt the Glory of the Lord.

After our trip to Wisconsin and our meeting with Caroline and Michael, our destination had become clear. We were positive that this baby was the one the Lord was speaking of five years prior on that old country road.

Scripture

Isaiah 40:3-5
In the wilderness prepare the way for the LORD; make straight in the desert highway for our God. Every valley shall be raised up, every mountain and hill made low; the rough ground shall become level, the rugged places a plain. And the glory of the LORD will be revealed, and all people will see it together. For the mouth of the LORD has spoken.

Thoughts Along the Way

If you have made contact with an expectant mother that you think could be "the one," what are the positive indicators that this is a good match for you? How do you see God's hand making "rugged places a plain" with this birth mother? Are there any concerns you still have about this particular birth mother? (Don't fret. There are usually a few.)

16

HEAD-HEART-HANDS

Financial Support to Your Birth Mom

Living in Maryland, we had few family members living close by. Most of our family lived on the West Coast, however, Joel's brother and his family lived in New Hampshire, which afforded us the joy of spending time with them more frequently. In the midst of our adoption, during a cold winter spell, Joel's brother, Jeff, flew down to spend a long weekend in Maryland.

As the kids were romping and wrestling with Joel and Jeff on the living room floor, the adoption phone rang. I grabbed the phone and ran upstairs, away from the giggling gaggle of bodies on the rug. Panting from my dash to the sanctuary of the upstairs bedroom, I trained my attention on the voice of Caroline. Her needs were as important as my needs or those of my family. I had grown to love Caroline as a person (irrespective of the fact that she was carrying my child), her welfare equaled that of the sweaty little ones wrestling downstairs.

Her voice trembled as she explained that she was behind on her heating bill and needed financial assistance to make it through this exceptionally cold winter. I asked her to read the latest bill. The words, "final notice" were enough for me to take immediate action.

I promised Caroline I would attend to the problem and would call her back when it was resolved. Making my promise reality was more complicated than I initially thought. I called for Joel, and he paused the monkey business to come upstairs and deal with a serious problem. He stood with hands at his sides, his face dripping with perspiration. I explained the situation and then called the utility company to make a payment to ensure their well-being.

I waited on hold for thirty minutes with the utility company while listening to elevator music, warped and distorted from miles of continuous play. The music was interrupted from time to time as a recorded voice told me that my call was important to the utility company. At last I heard another voice, this one a bit more spontaneous. In her greeting, she assured me that she would resolve my problem no matter what it might be. After I briefly explained the situation, she stated the company's strict policy never to discuss a customer's standing without consent received first from the customer and approved by the utility company. This bureaucratic script was obviously read off of her monitor, since her original sweet voice had turned into one of monotonous routine.

I quickly recognized that this situation was going to get ugly. I was not above pulling out my boxing gloves for this go 'round with the utility company. I was determined to get heat for Caroline, her family and my child. This is the set of circumstances we were up against: a by-the-book utility worker digging her heels into company policy, no function on our phones for 3-way calling, Caroline's limited minutes on her cell phone and a frigid home that was getting colder by the hour.

Stepping into the ring, I called Caroline on my cell, explained the situation and told her I would call her back on

Joel's phone once we had the company connected on my cell. It was my attempt at a 3-way call without official 3-way calling! We eventually got both parties on both lines, and Joel mashed the phones together in the palms of both hands. We could vaguely hear the representative explain the need for permission and then Caroline's response. Joel checked back in with the representative, she again explained her company's policy and she stressed she needed to *clearly* understand the account holder's permission (which was not fully understandable). My turn. "Caroline, she couldn't quite hear you," I said. "You may have to speak louder."

We embarked on Round Two. Joel forced the two cell phone receivers together like unwilling puzzle pieces, and we hoped that this second attempt would bring heat to our unborn daughter.

"Do you give permission to Joel England to discuss your account?" the company representative asked.

We could hear Caroline's clear response: "Yes."

Yet the agent was still not completely convinced.

I got back into the corner of the ring and coached Caroline to throw away all indiscretion by yelling her response. Round Three had commenced. Like Groundhog Day, the company representative repeated her spiel, but this time Caroline came out strong with a right hook, shouting a reverberating, "Yes!"

Then came the vanilla-sweet voice of the company representative who now spoke to Joel. At last she was willing to accept our payment of the bill. Joel, being a more cordial person than I, thanked her for her help.

Score for our babe and Caroline; they were going to be warm tonight!

As Joel and I high-fived each other, my peripheral vision picked up on an extra set of eyes. Jeff was a witness to our victory. For a moment I stepped into the shoes of an observer to this scene. I was made acutely aware of how this situation may look, especially to Jeff, who owns a car dealership. If anyone would be skeptical of persons attempting to scam, cheat or get by with a "good deal," it was Jeff. I was rewinding our celebration of success - making a payment to our birth mom - whom we had only been in contact with for a few months. We had no guarantees about the adoption and only verbal agreements with our birth mom. Jeff never questioned our efforts; in fact, he was whole-heartedly supportive and interested in our calling to adopt. But in that moment of reflection, I could see how an onlooker might raise a skeptical eyebrow at our utility payment.

Money and adoption as concepts don't seem to go together; there is a natural resistance to the merging of these two elements. Like oil and water, one would think these two areas are not compatible. However, money and adoption form a necessary relationship, a marriage even, that cannot be avoided. Many starting off on the road to adoption try to elope and avoid the money-adoption connection. Trust me, they do not get far.

One question that many people have asked us post-adoption is, "Did you pay your birth mom?" The choice of the word "pay" is interesting, and I believe is illustrative of an enormous misunderstanding in adoption. Normally, we give money in exchange for an item or service. This is true in adoption as well. You pay an attorney for his or her legal advice. You pay an agency for social work services, training and counseling. You pay the courts for their time. However, one thing you do *not* do is pay a birth mom for her child. Let me explain.

As I shared in an earlier chapter, every state has its own laws regarding how much an adoptive couple can support their birth mom financially. In some states it is virtually unlimited, and in others it is not allowed at all. Most states fall somewhere in the middle, permitting some support but capping the financial allowances. The state in which we adopted allowed for up to $5,000 in expenses to be paid to the birth mom. These contributions had to be in direct support of the unborn child. For example, we could help buy groceries or pay a heating bill, but we couldn't contribute to car expenses or toys for their other children.

In our preparation for adoption, this aspect of the process scared me. I did not want to become money-entangled by contributing financially to a birth mom I had only recently met and had no contractual assurances with regarding an unborn child.

But that was before we met Caroline. Her beautiful smile and soft heart ushered me into a relationship with a woman who was doing the right thing in a desperate circumstance. Her pregnancy became mine. Her hunger became my child's need for nourishment. Her stress was my child's stress. Caroline's inability to pay her heating bill became my child's unmet need for heat during a freezing winter. As implausible as it may seem, oil and water mixed. I went from being a leery potential adoptive parent to a protective mother.

As an adoptive mother, the toughest part of this process for me was not having control. The pregnancy was not mine, but I had already assumed the protective nature of a mother. The stress, nourishment and even toxins that the baby was exposed to in utero were completely out of my hands. That was a difficult reality to accept. But the fact that I was able to buy groceries at the end of the month when Caroline's resources ran dry or provide her with access to a cell phone for doctor calls and emergencies were huge sources of comfort for me.

Money and adoption do not have to be taboo subjects. It is a matter of perspective. When we look at adoption through the lens of the Lord, He clearly wants us to help others with our resources. Your purpose and who you are as a Christian are demonstrated through your actions. In James 2:15-17, this scenario is presented, "Suppose a brother or a sister is without clothes and daily food. If one of you says to them, "Go in peace; keep warm and well fed," but does nothing about their physical needs, what good is it? In the same way, faith by itself, if it is not accompanied by action, is dead."

I believe the entirety of adoption is faith in action.

One of our pastors once wisely said, "Your faith starts in your head as believing that there is a God, moves to your heart when you come into relationship with the Lord and then migrates to your hands as you act on your faith." Head-Heart-Hands. Before this journey is over, you may need a hydrating manicure for all the faith work being done by your hands.

Scripture

James 2:15-17
Suppose a brother or a sister is without clothes and daily food. If one of you says to them, "Go in peace; keep warm and well fed," but does nothing about their physical needs, what good is it? In the same way, faith by itself, if it is not accompanied by action, is dead.

Thoughts Along the Way

Can you recall a time in your life that you felt as if you were not in control? If so, how did you deal with that situation? What can you learn from that situation moving forward into this one?

17

PIXELATED PENCIL

Sound Words from a Christian Friend

Nothing made my heart beat faster than the sound of my adoption phone. As a psychology instructor, one of my favorite concepts to teach is classical conditioning. Ivan Pavlov, a Russian psychologist, was studying dogs and salivation. While it is probably not a shock to most, dogs salivate in response to the smell and sight of a piece of meat. But what Pavlov discovered was that if he repeatedly created a sound, such as a ringing bell, immediately prior to presenting the meat, the dogs would eventually salivate just to the sound of the bell. Bell rings, meat follows, dog salivates. Bell rings, meat follows, dog salivates. Eventually, Pavlov rang the bell and the dog salivated—even without the presence of meat.

Just like Pavlov's dog, I was classically conditioned to the sound of my adoption phone. Caroline's voice sent my heart pounding. For obvious reasons, I felt excited and anxious at the same time when I heard her sweet voice. Just as Pavlov's experiment demonstrated, I, too—after a few pairings of the ringtone and then hearing Caroline's voice—felt my heart pound and palms sweat only to the ringtone. In retrospect, I should have set the ringtone on my cell to "I'm so Excited" by the Pointer Sisters or Richard Marx's "Right Here Waiting for You." Actually, the tune that may best have matched my response was the theme song from "Jaws." Regardless, when that phone rang, my body's anxiety response system swung into full effect.

A few months out from the birth of our babe, the Pavlovian bell rang. This time, however, Caroline's contact was in the form of a text. To my glorious surprise, it was a picture of Caroline's belly! She was so considerate to send us a picture of her pregnant belly—our child growing inside of her. Her ability to see past her own crushing issues was a sign of her incredible strength and courage. The picture was a bit grainy but, sure enough, there was a belly that was getting larger. I could have stared at that picture all day long. Actually, I *did* stare at the picture all day long! I lingered over every pixel of that image. The fact is, you don't have many tangibles in adoption. If I could have eaten that photo, it would have been tremendous nourishment.

Something in the picture caught my eye, however. It was a long slender object behind Caroline's ear. Was it a pencil or a cigarette? The panic immediately set in. I pointed out the object in question to a neighbor. "What do you think?" She was unsure but expressed deep concern. Questions about my baby's health suddenly permeated my mind. All day, I ruminated over whether a blurry object in my prized picture was a pencil or cigarette.

My stomach tight and thoughts obsessive, I prayed. Even if the Lord had yelled his response into my ear, I would not have heard it over my own pervasive self-talk. I had all day to myself, as my kids were at school. Waiting outside of the school at pick-up, I was relieved to see my good friend, Carol. She is sensible, kind and quite honestly one of the wisest women I know. We met at our church and happened to also share a backyard fence, which made playdates with our two same-age, like-minded boys quite easy. I hurried over to her side to seek her advice on the picture. She carefully inspected it and was also unable to come to a concrete conclusion on the fuzzy object. I shared with Carol my deepest concern that our baby may be exposed to toxins in utero that could hinder normal development. I expressed my frustration with not being in control.

Carol spoke advice that I believe came straight from the Lord. She said, "Isn't that why you are adopting?" Her words took my breath away and jerked my head out of its negativity. She had taken my narrow focus and zoomed out to change my perspective. Whether that picture revealed a cigarette or pencil was irrelevant. The fact is that the Lord, Caroline and I all knew that Caroline's current life situation was not optimal for a baby. My purpose, through fulfilling God's calling, was to place this child into an enriched environment in which he or she could thrive. Trusting that the Lord would provide us the skills and the resources to do that became my prayer for that day.

I was so concerned with the appearance of a few pixels that I overlooked the big picture. It was the words of my true sister-in-Christ that helped me through a tough spot that day.

My circle of social support includes friends of many faiths, all of which I appreciate and respect. The point I want to make here is one of *inclusivity* not exclusivity. It is critical that your circle of social support *include* Christian friends who understand your faith and share in your love for Christ. I believe that the Lord can speak through others, and those words Carol spoke that day were God-inspired.

In James 3:17, it states: "The wisdom that comes from heaven is first of all pure; then peace-loving, considerate, submissive, full of mercy and good fruit, impartial, and sincere." Carol took me from a pixelated perspective to a heavenly vantage point because her counsel was Christ-centered. When others are providing advice to you, solicited or unsolicited, a biblically solid "checklist" to run through to assess the validity of their input is:

Is what they are offering up to you:

- Peace-loving?
- Considerate?
- Submissive?
- Full of Mercy?
- Impartial?
- Sincere?

Having a core support system is incredibly valuable. Let me revert once more to the wise words of our adoption attorney, Mark, who said, "If you want to adopt, you *will* adopt. Adoption is certain, you just have to hang in there long enough." Much of the "hanging in there" part of the equation is having kind, wise and faith-filled friends who can boost you through the tough spots. If you already have a core group of people to whom you can turn, you are in good position. If however, you are feeling a need for more support, I encourage you to join a Bible Study at a local church, get connected and share your story. It won't be long before people flock to your aid. The Lord wants to surround you with His living angels, but you need to open yourself up to those friendships and their support. Thank the Lord for the Carols of this world!

Scripture

James 3:17
The wisdom that comes from heaven is first of all pure; then peace-loving, considerate, submissive, full of mercy and good fruit, impartial and sincere.

Thoughts Along the Way

Who are your most trusted friends who can support you on this journey? If they are far from you, what are ways that you can reach out to receive their wise and loving counsel?

18

GLORIOUS SIGNING

The Importance of Worship

There is a push and pull in my life that has led to several folks not wanting to sit by me in church. One, I have a horrible voice. Two, I love worship music. Perhaps the Lord saw this and intervened in the most witty way. Let me explain.

Our sixth Air Force assignment was to Mountain Home, Idaho—population 5,000—the same place the Lord called us to adopt on the old country road. Obviously, in hindsight, I am grateful for that placement. As we drove into town for the first time, the GPS voice with a British accent in our Honda CRV—packed to the brim with our most treasured belongings including two children in their car seats—chirped, "You have arrived." I distinctly remember asking, "Arrived where? There is nothing here." The nothingness that I first perceived did turn out to be something, but it was a sparse something. Here's an idea…let's not call a town Mountain Home when there are no mountains nearby.

Aside from the dismal aesthetics, I quickly discovered that there were few programs and activities available for kids. We tried horseback riding at a local ranch, but when I heard gunshots and found empty bullet casings near the trail where my daughter was riding, I reconsidered her equestrian future. I started seeking opportunities for my kids that were not part of a formal program.

As we sat in church one Sunday morning, I noticed a teenage girl signing, not singing, along with the worship songs. It was quite possibly one of the most beautiful and powerful moments of worship I had ever witnessed. My eyes could not part from her expressive hands signing the songs. A light bulb turned on in my brain; my dramatic and faithful Kelsey could learn praise sign.

Over the course of the next year, she learned praise songs with Melissa, a quiet mannered, fiercely faithful high school student. The first song she put hands to was "How Great Thou Art." Joel was, at the time, deployed to Qatar in the Middle East. Since Skype constantly froze, I sent him videos of the kids each month. The Easter video featured Kelsey praising the Lord with this song, her actions as beautiful as the words. Wow, talk about tears.

My initial quest was to find Kelsey an activity through which she could learn and grow, but in reality *I* started to learn and grow right alongside her. We both had an excitement for praise sign that held on long after we moved from Mountain Home. We became YouTube praise sign students and taught it to others as we bumped along our Air Force road. At the Christian women's conferences, I sought out the deaf section and sat close by to praise among those signing.

My worship dilemma was finally solved. I could praise the Lord with such fervor and not offend the person sitting next to me with my off-key notes. I found that even when I was at the gym listening to my worship music on the elliptical, I was simultaneously praising with my hands. Forget pumping the handles, I was just pumping up the Lord. Plus, I was already sweaty and stinky—might has well add in a little "crazy" for onlookers.

"Glorious" is my favorite sign. It starts with both arms extended out in front of your body. One arms remains extended and the other then arches like a rainbow with the hand rotating back and forth. I had never before been able to express with words how I felt inside while signing. "Glorious" changed that for me. One word-in-action finally matched my emotion for the love and awe I feel for our Lord.

Christian music and worship were absolute necessities throughout our adoption. In the car, during my exercise time (which was inconsistent but important), and at home, praise music gave me focus and relief from the stress of everyday life happenings and the adoption. Any opportunity that came along to attend a Bible study or go to a women's conference, I jumped on. Part of my motivation to attend these events was that there would be built-in worship time. I knew that I had to be full in order to be able to give what I was about to give.

There are all kinds of ways to praise the Lord in worship. Psalm 150 teaches us that praise can come in varying forms.

> Praise the LORD.
> Praise God in his sanctuary;
> praise him in his mighty heavens.
> Praise him for his acts of power;
> praise him for his surpassing greatness.
> Praise him with the sounding of the trumpet,
> praise him with the harp and lyre,
> Praise him with timbrel and dancing,
> praise him with the strings and pipe,
> Praise him with the clash of cymbals,
> praise him with resounding cymbals.
> Let everything that has breath praise the LORD.

When we glorify God we *find* Him. On a run, in a stadium, in a sanctuary, in the driver's seat, on the elliptical, He speaks through the words of worship songs. Sing, sign, or maybe play an instrument, and thank Him for what he is doing in your life. Even through songs you've heard a hundred times, you might find that all of a sudden a lyric pops out like a highlighted word on a page. He is working His way in you through worship. Praise is powerful.

I wanted to give you a start to an adoption praise playlist. Most of these songs were included on my "Ali's Adoption Playlist" that kept me sane and serving our Lord on our adoption journey.

Meant to Be, Steven Curtis Chapman
Dive, Steven Curtis Chapman
Be Still and Know, Steven Curtis Chapman
Hallelujah, You are Good, Steven Curtis Chapman
Letters, Kelsey England
My Deliverer, Mandisa
Sweeter, Travis Cottrell
Shackles, Mary Mary
God is Great, Travis Cottrell
Good Morning, Mandisa & TobyMac
Just Be Held, Casting Crowns
While I'm Waiting, John Waller
Indescribable, Chris Tomlin
Blessings, Laura Story
Glorious Day, Casting Crowns
Bring the Rain, MercyMe
Better Than a Hallelujah, Amy Grant
Praise You in This Storm, Casting Crowns
Thy Will Be Done, Hillary Scott

Be sure your journey includes praise music. It will be a sustaining force in this pursuit.

Scripture

Psalms 150
Praise the LORD.
Praise God in his sanctuary;
praise him in his mighty heavens.
Praise him for his acts of power;
praise him for his surpassing greatness.
Praise him with the sounding of the trumpet,
praise him with the harp and lyre,
Praise him with timbrel and dancing,
praise him with the strings and pipe,
Praise him with the clash of cymbals,
praise him with resounding cymbals.
Let everything that has breath praise the LORD.

Thoughts Along the Way

What are your favorite worship songs? Steven Curtis Chapman's song, "Dive", was my theme song for our adoption. If you haven't made a dedicated playlist of worship songs for your adoption, do that now!

Go to YouTube and search "Here I Am to Worship in ASL & CC by Rock Church Deaf Ministry." Challenge yourself to learn a few signs, then when you are overwhelmed by the glory of God you can just shout with your hands everything you feel!

19

CANYON

Empathizing with Your Birth Mom

Headphones on, praise music pumping, I gripped the arm rest for take-off on my second trip to Wisconsin. Just two months earlier, Joel and I had made our first trip to meet Caroline and Michael. The priceless time spent with them splashing in the pool, making playdough pancakes and gathering around family photo albums in the hotel lobby cemented our commitment to one another. I was flying solo this trip since Joel was needed at home to coach the kids' soccer games and attend Kelsey's violin recital.

Landing in Milwaukee, my mind shifted into high gear as I slid into my rental car. Caroline had invited me to join her for the ultrasound, scheduled for the next day, and today I would spend a few hours with them at their home. I had not gone far when I turned on the air conditioning. Wisconsin in mid-September clings to its summer heat and moisture. School had begun, and I was often slowed by yellow school buses picking up groups of kids who, only two weeks into the school year, already boarded the buses with reluctance.

Driving through the small mid-western town was like entering another world. My home lay between Washington D.C. and Baltimore. Not far from our home was the United States Naval Academy and close by was Fort Meade, home of the National Security Agency. Across the Potomac River was the Pentagon. Joel's office was at Andrews Air Force Base, but he was often called upon to work at the Pentagon.

My life buzzed in the midst of the nation's business. It was fast-paced, and I struggled to balance my responsibilities as an instructor at the community college, an involved mom and a supportive spouse.

I looked out the window of my rental car at sleepy little rural villages, with stores along a single street and old men sitting on benches in green-grass parks. Smoke rose from their pipes, echoing the town's pace. The towns I drove through were similar to one another, with only a few people walking slowly on cracked sidewalks next to empty, diagonal parking spaces.

I wondered. What would their home be like? What do their struggles look like, those struggles that have led them to the platform of adoption? My social worker's instincts knew to be prepared for heartache. I followed my GPS, glad it was audibly giving directions because I could only occasionally glance at the screen between dodging potholes.

I pulled up to a two-story wooden home. All the suggestions of poverty were present: peeling paint, broken porch rails and patched windows. On both sides of the front walkway sat weeds that had survived the summer heat. It was a rental, and the landlord had clearly given up on any sort of maintenance. A man I didn't recognize was smoking in a randomly placed chair on the side of the home. For a moment, I questioned whether or not this was the correct address. But, soon enough, I heard the voices of children and was assured I was standing in the yard of my child's birth mom. The steps to the front porch sagged from years of traffic, and I watched my footing as I looked for a doorbell that had long since died of old age. The inner door was swung open to afford a hopeful breeze of relief from the oppressive heat. Through the screen door I called, "Anyone home? Hello!"

From the kitchen came Caroline with her radiant smile, and my trepidation eased. She was like a diamond reflecting light in a dark room. She swung the screen door open for me to enter. It dragged on its one remaining hinge, but Caroline ignored the decay of her surroundings. She was somehow able to live above the conditions that poverty brought.

As a professional social worker, I had been able to maintain a psychological distance from those to whom I was offering help. But Caroline was a part of me. My gut wrenched, and I wanted to cry. I wanted to throw my arms around her and tell her that I would fix it, that she was going to have only the good things in life. The legal constraint that I could not exceed $5,000 in financial support loomed in my mind. I said little, trying to measure every word. I had to resist the urge to speak from my heart, as I would surely promise more than I could legally deliver. I was overwhelmed in the moment, considering this person who had so much virtue while drowning in problems not of her making.

Facing eviction for nonpayment of rent, this home, too, would probably be only temporary. What lay beyond was unknown. I asked myself how it was that a person could survive in such a chaos of instability.

I looked around the living room. On an entertainment system were framed photographs of family members. I examined each photo, and Caroline proudly pointed to the photo of her grandparents, school portraits of her children, and the picture of her and her mother.

Her youngest was not even a year old, and with only two bedrooms in the house, a crib was standing in a corner of the living room. Caroline explained that a friend had given her the crib. It was probably from the 1970s with wooden bars, and it was missing a foot castor. That leg was propped up by books to keep the crib level. While continuing the conversation, Caroline returned to the kitchen to make the baby a bottle. As she opened the refrigerator, I caught a quick glimpse of its sparse shelves.

I sat on the floor and Caroline and Michael's oldest child sat next to me. He showed me his favorite toys. I pulled him closer to me and admired his collection, examining each one and asking him which was his favorite.

As I sat in the midst of their difficulty, to be completely truthful, a part of me wanted to flee back to my suburban home. Yet another part of me felt as though I never wanted to leave Caroline's side. I could not help but feel guilty about my lifestyle in the face of her day-to-day struggles. That guilt stung because I knew that in less than 24 hours I would leave without wholly fixing this situation.

I rose from the floor, asked Caroline which grocery store she preferred and purchased a gift card for her to use as needed. She nodded in humble gratitude as she changed the baby's diaper.

Here we were, two women solidly connected by a common goal—to ensure the well being of this unborn child. Yet, the canyon that separated our circumstances was deep and wide. How could I empathize with my birth mom when I was on the receiving end of her loss? I had not fully anticipated this challenge. Not only were we coming from different places but the outcome of our connection would leave us on different planes— mine of gain and hers of loss.

This dilemma brought to mind Carl Rogers, one of my favorite psychologists, who clarified the meaning of empathy.

> "To be with another in this way means that for the time being you lay aside the views and values you

> hold for yourself in order to enter another's world without prejudice. In some sense it means that you lay aside your self; and this can only be done by a person who is secure enough in themselves that they know they will not get lost in what may turn out to be the strange or bizarre world of the other, and they can comfortably return to his own world when they wish. Perhaps this description makes clear that being empathic is a complex, demanding, strong-yet also a subtle and gentle-way of being."[1]

This was my challenge. I had to put aside my views and values and step into Caroline's shoes, free of prejudice. What made this more difficult was that I was barely fitting into my *own* shoes as a first-time adoptive parent.

The role that you assume as adoptive parent requires an empathy toward your birth mom. Trust begins when one person believes the other understands. Encouraging her that this decision she is making is selfless and valued will be critical for you to get across. One tip I can offer is to write down the thoughts that you most want to communicate prior to meeting or talking on the phone. I found that having my thoughts clear helped me not to get off track and prohibited my emotions from clouding what I really intended to say.

Still, no depth of understanding or empathizing on my part could equal the needs she would have for support after the baby was born. One of the biggest reasons we felt our adoption was a success was because of the loving support Caroline had from her own mother. I was positive that Caroline would be held in Julia's loving arms after this child was born and placed into ours.

Ensuring that your birth mom has a social support system in place is, hands down, one of the most influential factors in a successful adoption. This support system will be the safety net for her and your adoption through the emotionally charged and difficult parts, like the first few days after birth and the signing of the termination of parental rights papers. In fact, research finings point to the signing of the termination of parental rights papers as one of the most difficult for birth mothers. Researchers from Columbia University, Cushman and Kalmuss found:

> Over half of birth moms, "rated the actual signing of papers as more difficult than several other potentially difficult points in time, such as the last months of pregnancy, the first few days after the birth…The authors speculate that signing the surrender papers constitutes the end point of an often difficult decision making process; indeed, signing the papers transforms the adoption "plan" into a reality. It thus seems apparent that young relinquishers need a great deal of emotional support at that stage of the adoption process."[2]

Understanding what parts of the adoption process might be most difficult for your birth mother will better enable you to be empathetic to her needs. The relationship you build with your birth mom will be the most important asset in your successful adoption!

While Rogers is an authority on empathy, let's turn our eyes to our God, who is *the* authority. Rogers cites an important truth: emotional support of your birth mom will be demanding. But in Philippians 4:13 we are reminded, "I can do all this through him who gives me strength." There were several points in our adoption, either in phone conversations with Caroline or in face-to-face discussions, when my head was nodding and my face was smiling, but my mind was silently reciting that scripture as I mentally scrambled to communicate the right words of support to our birth mom.

In those moments of complexity when you are unsure what to say next, be comforted that, "it is God who works in you to will and to act in order to fulfill his good purpose." (Philippians 2:13) The Holy Spirit is working behind the scenes as you step out in faith. God has such a phenomenal purpose in mind for you; the words you say and hoops you jump through will fulfill His mighty will for you, your birth mom and your child. Rest assured that although you might feel like you are muddling through a particular conversation with your birth mom, those words are healing and encouraging nourishment that have been masterfully prepared by the Lord himself.

Scripture

Philippians 4:13
I can do all this through him who gives me strength.

Philippians 2:13
It is God who works in you to will and to act in order to fulfill his good purpose.

Thoughts Along the Way

Draw a circle around your birth mom. Now brainstorm to make a list of all the people you know of who support her in this adoption decision. There is not a lot you can do to alter that picture. You can certainly pencil in yourself as a support. You might also be able to add a counselor or social worker but, in the hospital, there needs to be someone in addition to you because the hard fact is that you will leave with a baby, and she will not. From the start, a birth mom with a strong social network surrounding her is a good indicator that the adoption will not fall through.

20

ULTRASOUND

Joy of All Joys

September 9, 2011

I saw you today! My precious little GIRL! Your birth mom's feeling was right; you are a girl. What a wiggler you are, non-stop I tell you. I am a bit jealous that I can't feel all that movement. You cooperated though so we could find out your gender; thank you! Caroline and I held hands, mesmerized by you for almost 45 minutes. Tears streamed down our faces. We were in awe of you. I giggled a lot, too. It was that giggle of disbelief. I could hardly believe I was seeing you, my child, for the very first time. "Amazing" is all I can say!

Your little hand covered your face a few times and pushed that ultrasound tech's instrument away. You are already letting people know what you like and don't like. Way to stand up for yourself! I loved seeing your brain. You know that is the part of you that really makes you who you will become. I'm going to bring back pictures and show you off to my developmental psychology students, as any proud mom would.

Your heartbeat was the sweetest sound, too. I wish the ultrasound tech had stayed on it all day for me to just absorb that sound into my innermost being. You were opening and closing your mouth, tasting all the goodness of Caroline's nourishment. Your birth mom is a salsa lover (like Alex); maybe you will love it, too?

You know, today was hard for your birth mom. She is an extremely strong woman. I hope you take after her in that way. To see such a precious life growing inside her and still have the strength to see beyond this day and this month, takes a MIGHTY strong woman. She loves you so much and wants only the very best for you. I am beyond honored that she sees us as the very best for you.

I wish I could fast forward 6 months and hold you in my arms. There is a lot of time between now and Jan. 21 (your due date), and then, even after, we will have to wait to ensure you are legally truly ours. That is a lot of waiting for this mama! God put you in my heart 5 years ago, and today was the day I finally got to see your beautiful face. Ahhhh, now to just hold you, and then I will be complete. Our family will be complete. God's calling for us will be fulfilled, and you, my darling daughter, will be unconditionally loved for the rest of your earthly life.

Oh, today was BIG. I am blessed. I will go to bed tonight with my cheeks hurting from a perpetual smile. The joy in my heart is overflowing. I could have sat there all day, watching you move, adoring your cute little self. The magnitude of this gift we are receiving from your birth mom is indescribable. I will always ensure that you know what an unselfish and loving person she is.

Love, Mom

PS- I talked to Caroline about your name. She was so gracious and wants you to have "England" as your last name from birth. I shared with her how I loved the name "Annika." It means "sweet faced; God has favored me." Amanda agreed that it is a beautiful name.

Now back to staring at your pictures, Annika England.

After all my pondering, planning and searching, I laid eyes on my baby. While there was no burning bush, God made space for an answer in a hushed ultrasound room, in the grasp of two women holding hands. Our tears, an equal mix of joy and heartache, seemed to seal our connection and plans for this adoption. It turned out that day that I did not have to step into anyone's shoes or think clinically about empathetic words. We were simply connected, on the same page, wanting the same thing: love for this unborn child.

Habakkuk writes, "I will climb up into my watchtower now and wait to see what the LORD will say to me and how he will answer my complaint." Habakkuk's expectation was that he would receive answers from the Lord. My baby's face was God's answer, and my giggle reflected my pure giddiness in his reply.

We can learn from Habakkuk. One, take the time to be alone. Two, present your questions to the Lord. Three, expect to receive answers. I heard the Lord's calling on an old country road. I then spent five years asking and seeking from my watchtower. And finally on that ultrasound day, I received what I was looking for. I saw my baby!

Scripture

Habakkuk 2:1 (NLT)
I will climb up into my watchtower now and wait to see what the LORD will say to me and how he will answer my complaint.

Thoughts Along the Way

Where is your watchtower? It is a quiet place in your home, or a nearby park, or your backyard? Habakkuk knew it was important to get away from people and gain perspective. Identify a place and commit to spending some time in that space just asking and listening to your Lord. Then wait.

21

SANDY MOAT

Establishing Trust Through Understanding

My mom's house in Newport Beach was my home as a young child and during my school years, and has continued to be my second home throughout my life as an adult. It has afforded me the opportunity to share experiences with my children that I had as a child. Pulling a red wagon filled with sand toys, towels and a few snacks, with a light heart I take my children down to the same beach I played on, just a few short blocks from my mom's house.

Of course, building sandcastles was a craft I had honed over many years as a beach rat and one I was excited to share with Alex. Alex is my industrious child. He is a builder, so on this particular day we chatted about our plans to build a mighty castle with a moat. We used our colorful plastic shovels and pails to craft a magnificent structure. We decorated with shells and even added a little mud drip on the top for added height.

We spoke in Knights of Old lingo (really, just a British accent with a few thus-es and thous thrown in), and arduously protected our castle from the nasty bands of heathens who brought destruction and mayhem. The king's answer to such peril was a deep moat around the castle. It would be filled with water and was impassable except by way of a drawbridge. So, we dug a deep trench all around our sandcastle.

It was Alex's job to run down to the water and fill a pail with water to fill the moat. He is an active boy, so I knew this exhausting venture would be good for him. He toddled down to the water's edge, scooped up a pail full of salt water and delicately tiptoed back up the sandy hill to dump his fetch in the moat. For a brief moment, it was perfect. Then, disappointment spread across Alex's face as the water absorbed into the sandy earth. His natural reaction was to quickly run down to the ocean to refill his moat. Again, the thirsty grains of sand quickly drank up the water. It only took a few moments for gravity to do its job. No matter how many times he would refill, or how quickly he could make that round trip to the shoreline, the moat would not retain the water. So we pretended that the moat was full of water and let the dark stain of moisture serve as that water. We stepped back from our masterpiece to admire our attention to detail. Turrets defied the sun's rays and stood proudly. I think Alex could see the knights in the courtyard and the archers on the pulpits sending lethal arrows down on the invaders.

It is inevitable that, as an adoptive parent, you will want to support and fill the needs of your birth mother. It is a natural reaction to want to run, and get, and give whatever need you see unfulfilled and fill it. As our birth family's needs became known to us, we naturally wanted to help. I wanted nothing more than to see Caroline and Michael climb out of the depths of poverty.

As tempted as you may be to believe that your short-term financial contributions may make a difference, realize that they will most likely only be a Band-Aid covering a much larger and deeper wound. It is important to understand that there are limits to how much you can help (dictated by state law) and ways in which your help might be most effective.

When I was a graduate student at the University of Hawaii Social Work School, I interned at a local hospital. Working with patients, I did what Alex did, tirelessly ran to fill a moat with water. I was exposed to people with such difficult circumstances, and my tendency was to want to fix their problems. I heard "I'm hungry," and my mind immediately went to all the community food banks and soup kitchens. I heard "I'm depressed," and I racked my brain for referrals to counselors who specialized in cognitive-behavioral therapy. Over time, I learned that while those referrals and crisis actions were important, their impact was short-lived. Long-term solutions required more listening and deeper understanding of the issues that brought my clients to their respective circumstances. What I thought was a perfectly logical solution may not have been received as such by my clients. I learned over time that the most important catalyst for change was my relationship with the client. Building trust was crucial to affecting change.

I deeply encourage you to establish trust as your priority with your birth family. Follow through with whatever you say you will do. Words supported by action are a good start. To do that requires knowledge and understanding, and that can only happen through listening. So, less talking and more listening is a good rule of thumb.

We learned an incredible amount in our first meeting with our birthparents. For example, both our birthparents were unemployed when we met them. Without context to their situation, one might assume that they were lazy or unskilled. As we got to know our birth father, he revealed some interesting insights. He was from a bad area in a big city, but had relocated to the small town in which we met him. This small town was primarily Caucasian, and not terribly friendly to African Americans. He had been a victim of discrimination, which had thwarted his efforts to find employment. The jobs he could get were temporary and short-term, such as stocking shelves. He shared with us that he did not finish high school. While he did not try to explain away his school-related failures, we began to see a fuller picture of a man who grew up in poverty, had a learning disability that went undetected for much too long, received few support services from the school and had zero academic support at home. It was the perfect recipe to create a high school drop out. To a large extent, he was failed by his family, his community and society as a whole. As we empathized with our birth father's dire circumstance, a deep sadness came over us.

Listening is the critical first step, but following close behind is the importance of taking notes of what is said. I know it seems clinical, but because our own thoughts and emotions are so intense, it is important to write down what a birth mom and father say. These are a few comments that our birth mom shared that I jotted down:

- I don't want to be alone with the baby in the hospital; I want Joel and you there.
- If the baby gets hurt or has a medical condition, I want to know about it.
- I want to hear and see how excited you are, talking about names or decorating the nursery.
- This baby is yours; it is my gift to you.

Writing down her wishes and thoughts helped me to better understand her perspective. I was able to commit her comments to memory. I then could reassure her that we would meet these specific needs.

In addition, I wrote down words that I wanted to clearly communicate to our birth mom:

- We think of you and are praying for you each day and our beautiful daughter.
- Your decision to adopt is selfless not selfish!
- I will share with this child your heart for her, the heart that has given us a chance to grow as a loving family, and I will let her know that she can love you and be grateful to you also.
- We plan to tell this child all about you, how kind, unselfish and loving you are.
- Your gift to us is the most priceless and precious gift we have ever received.

The "whens" of communication are determined mostly by the birth mother. While I strategically timed my phone calls so that I was in a quiet place with my thoughts together, incoming calls from our birth mother came at many inopportune times. Still, wherever I was, no matter what I was doing, I answered the phone and gave her my full attention. I had more than one Walmart conversation. With two kids in tow and "we need an aisle 3 cleanup" blaring over the speaker, I struggled to be attentive. With my eyes shut and a finger closing my other ear, I did what I needed to so that I could focus and listen to her.

The adoption phone once rang when we were at an aquarium while on vacation. I found myself quickly wiping fish guts off my hands (we were feeding seals with the kids). If you have ever heard a seal bark, it's no-joke loud. Answering the phone, I begin to hear Caroline explaining to me about contractions and doctor's appointments, all the while I was trying to flag down my kids to cease throwing fish to the noisy seals. Comical and stressful, these will be some of your Johnnie-Walker Red moments.

Our scripture tells us that, "Wisdom is found on the lips of a person who has understanding." (Proverbs 10:13) My friend, as you navigate the uncharted territory of this newfound relationship, I encourage you first to listen. Gain understanding of where your birth mother and birth father are coming from. Resist the urge to fix and fill because it is from a point of understanding that you can connect and speak words of wisdom that will establish a caring and life-long relationship.

Scripture

Proverbs 10:13 (GW)
Wisdom is found on the lips of a person who has understanding.

Thoughts Along the Way

Do you have a journal or notebook to keep all your thoughts in one central place? You may want to designate a folder or notebook for your thoughts. Writing down the important ones is your only real defense against forgetting them.

22

HIT THE FLOOR

When an Expectant Mom Changes Her Mind

Here we go into the dreaded chapter that addresses the "what if" of an expectant mother changing her mind. I want to keep the focus positive and encourage you that many people adopt without ever experiencing an adoption fall-through. But I also want to paint an accurate picture of adoption, and the fact is, some people encounter an expectant mom who changes her mind. Should this become part of your story, know that you are not alone! It is a rough spot, but if approached carefully, it can stand as simply a small detour, not a barricade.

When my husband puts on his lawyer hat and explains adoption to others, it sounds like this: "Adoption is all about minimizing risk in an inherently risky effort." It is Joel's job to analyze liability and risk. That is probably why he clung to the "Choosing Birth Parents: The Ten Red Flags" handout from the FPA handbook.[1] It was a helpful tool in determining the level of risk we assumed with each potential birth mother. While not a perfect assessment measure, it did provide us with focused considerations when selecting our birth mother.

Although prudent risk assessment is important, no one can fully predict the future decisions an expectant mother might make and how her circumstances may change over the course of her pregnancy. What I want to emphasize is, if an expectant mother has a change of mind, *it has nothing to do with you* and everything to do with her situation and the unexpected emotional overload.

One practical tip of which to be aware is there can sometimes be financial loss with a change in birth mothers, so be sure to look at the adoption tax credit for failed (I really do not like the word "failed," but that is the wording used within the tax law) adoptions. It can be very helpful!

I turned to an incredible adoptive parent and faith-filled woman, Sarah Thatcher, who was willing to share her story about the detour they experienced on their adoption path.

Sarah's Story

We connected with a birth mom through a mutual friend. The expectant mother was in a place, financially, where she could not care for the twins that she was expecting. She was seeking an adoption plan, but had gone to an agency and did not like the sterile feel of it, so when our mutual friend told her about us, she was willing to meet us.

A couple of weeks later, she waddled into our home at 6 months pregnant and we got to know each other. We talked about our lives, her three other kids, parenting, our stories, the story of how Caleb and I started dating, pregnancy, motherhood, real life. After about three hours of tears, laughs and conversation in-between, the birth mom said something like "I have been looking for a couple that I am comfortable with and that I connect with as a family to raise these babies. I like you guys and your personalities and I would love for you to be their parents."

I immediately jumped up, and held onto this sweet mama who CHOSE US! We cried together and just sat in that moment for a while.

Caleb cried, I cried (and screamed....because that's what I do when I am excited!) and I think she got to know us even more in that moment.

Through our excitement, I thought about her and her heart that is struggling and in pain and over and over again I kept telling her how sorry I was that this is so tough for her. I can't imagine.

She is a mom to three boys. She loves being a mom. She didn't want to do this but out of love for these babies, she decided this was the best route, not out of irresponsibility, but out of responsibilty to do what is best for them because the situation that she was currently in, wasn't best. I just remember thinking how brave she was.

Over the next few weeks after we announced our upcoming adoption of the twins, we were absolutely showered with hand-me-downs and gifts from so many generous people and in the meantime, we were getting to build a relationship with our birth mom. We adored her. It was amazing to me how quickly she had a place in our hearts and felt like part of our family. We were excited about the possibility of an open adoption with her, if she decided that was what she wanted. However, after our first doctor's visit with her, where we got to hear the two little heartbeats, our birth mom told us that she was having a tough time with the whole situation. She said that she wasn't changing her mind but asked for space.

That was a rough text to receive and fear and panic washed over me as I read it over and over again. I was so worried that she was going to change her mind and that these babies wouldn't be ours anymore. That very morning I remember praying and asking the Lord to refine me more before I became a mommy. Little did I know how quickly he would answer!

I was a mess for a few days and had to continually hand the fear I was feeling over to the Lord because I just couldn't handle it on my own. I wanted to trust her (our birth mom) when she said that she wasn't changing her mind. I wanted to trust what I saw in her situation when it looked impossible for her to keep these twins. I wanted to trust God that He had it all under control with my best in mind but it was a struggle!

Through the fear, we decided to continue preparing in every way for arrival of the twins. We decorated their little room and washed and organized all of their clothes and baby items. I was in my happy place because I got to get crafty and as I sewed, glued and designed, I would just pray for "our" twins and imagine them in our little red house. We had been debating over names for a few weeks but in this time of preparation, their names became clear to us. Once we named them, our prayers became more specific for each of them and their futures. This season of preparation was such a sweet one. Fear had eventually left and excitement jumped in.

But then….

This one particular morning I woke up and was finally able to emotionally hand the twins over to the Lord and really let go of control. (I didn't really have any anyway, but I tried to)! I was in a constant internal battle, trying to release control and this one morning, I was finally able to.

I sent a text to our birth mom to check in and ask for some information that we needed and I hit the floor when I read the first line:

"We have decided to keep the babies…..".

She continued on to explain that her situation had changed and therefore, they were going to keep them.

Here is the thing, I have hit the floor before. I have spent time on the floor writhing in pain, unable to control my emotions, body or thoughts and THAT is the very place I found true intimacy with Jesus. I grew up knowing who Jesus was but it wasn't until I was on the floor, alone, ten years ago that I first really met Him and felt Him. And because of His closeness in my life, from that very place years ago, the floor is actually a sweet place of rest for me.

I have prayed over and over again in the last 10 years to be able experience that same intimacy without the grief that brought me there and the truth is, I always get in my own way. So as I laid in the middle of the floor in my living room, although I was overcome with sadness and grief, I felt peace because there He was, my Father, holding me.

Now, that doesn't mean that I didn't feel the grief any less, I just wasn't alone in it. Caleb came home from work soon after that and we just held each other as we tried to comprehend what this meant for our family.

I got to see the birth mom the following day and that helped me, and I thank her too, so much. I still love her. I still love those twins because I'm invested in them. But I knew I had to fully let them go. God promises in Romans 8:28, "In all things God works for the good of those who love Him, who have been called according to His purpose." Since it wasn't good yet, I knew He wasn't finished yet. I knew that text was not the end of our adoption story!

The following months I found that Caleb and I both grieved so differently but our loss became a window through which we learned much about each other and grew together on a deeper level. We both decided to put a pause on everything adoption-related. We had to mourn the twins, and that took some time. We shut out the world and honed in on each other. I closed the door to the nursery with the two empty cribs.

Six weeks later (it felt a lot longer), we decided to again open our profile at the adoption agency. I was cognizant that the twins were not on my mind all the time anymore. The space happened. It felt good that the Lord had brought us so far in just a month and a half. I was surprised by how quickly our hearts recovered from such a deep wound.

Sarah's incredible strength and resilience in the face of such devastating loss is a feat of giants. Through her example we can learn a few things about how to make it through such a disappointing setback. Sarah took some important steps in order to move forward:

- She allowed herself to grieve-to hit the floor.
- She remembered an earlier time in her life when the Lord brought her through crisis and restored her wholly.
- She recalled scripture and listened to His Word.
- She got up.
- She paused for healing.
- She moved forward on the adoption path.

Sarah and her husband's ability to "hang in there" had everything to do with their hope in the Lord and belief in His promise. Nine months after Sarah lay sobbing on the floor, she and her husband were cuddling their adopted newborn baby boy.

Her description of "hitting the floor" still brings goose bumps to my arms. I have heard it said before: "When you are on the floor, at your lowest point, the only place you have to look is up." Sarah did more than look up, however. She allowed herself to be held by the Lord - right there on the floor.

When talking with Sarah, she shared a story from the Bible that gave her strength all along her adoption journey. It comes from Matthew 8:23-27:

> "Then he got into the boat and his disciples followed him. Suddenly a furious storm came up on the lake, so that the waves swept over the boat. But Jesus was sleeping. The disciples went and woke him, saying, "Lord, save us! We're going to drown!"
>
> He replied, "You of little faith, why are you so afraid?" Then he got up and rebuked the winds and the waves, and it was completely calm.
>
> The men were amazed and asked, "What kind of man is this? Even the winds and the waves obey him!"

You may relate to the feeling of sheer panic experienced when the winds of adoption whip up and the waves seem to come upon you. Like the disciples, you may even cry out to the Lord, "Hey, I am going to drown here!" What is critical to remember from this story is that the Lord calmed the storm, brought them across to their destination, unscathed. Log this message from the Lord in your brain: "I will get you across." The Lord can hush the winds and settle the seas, and he *will* get you across. Batten down the hatches, friend, you simply have to ride this one out.

Scripture

Romans 8:28
And we know that in all things God works for the good of those who love Him, who have been called according to His purpose.

Matthew 8:23-27
Then he got into the boat and his disciples followed him. Suddenly a furious storm came up on the lake, so that the waves swept over the boat. But Jesus was sleeping. The disciples went and woke him, saying, "Lord, save us! We're going to drown!"

He replied, "You of little faith, why are you so afraid?" Then he got up and rebuked the winds and the waves, and it was completely calm.

The men were amazed and asked, "What kind of man is this? Even the winds and the waves obey him!"

Thoughts Along the Way

Sarah's story brings adoptive parents' fears to the foreground. Your story may never take this detour, but if it does, know this: you are not alone. Look for resources that guide you in good risk assessment (that's the pedaling part), and then just ride it out in faith. I hope you caught the ending to her adoption journey…it's a good one! You can read more from Sarah's adoption path at her website inourlittleredhouse.com.[2]

23

ERIKSON AND IDENTITY

Our Choice for an Open Adoption

One of my toughest cases as a therapist was counseling a high school student I will call "Ron." His behavior suggested some deep-seated problems. Ron was on the verge of dropping out of high school but, even worse, he was engaging in criminal activity that was most likely going to land him in jail. I say jail because he had just turned 18, and he was, therefore, no longer eligible for juvenile detention. To most rational people, the prospect of going to jail would be such a deterrent that they would change their behavior in order to avoid such an unpleasant experience. I was shocked when Ron revealed his true indifference toward the prospect of having all freedom taken away and living in a cage.

I listened to his story, attempting to discover the cause of Ron's disillusionment. Once we got past his surface-level irritations with teachers the school administration and a few minor crises with his friends, he eventually got down to the core of his issues: he was adopted. However, Ron was not told he was adopted. When he was thirteen years old, a distant cousin, who knew his circumstances and assumed my client had been told of his adoption, informed him. Ron's identity was rocked; his world was shattered. All that he believed to be real and true was not. The well-intentioned shield his adoptive parents thought they provided was actually a sword only waiting to be wielded through a casual conversation with a cousin. Now, he was struggling with how to recreate his identity.

Erik Erikson is one of the most renowned theorists in Developmental Psychology. His eight-stage psychosocial developmental model is used in practice as one of the most comprehensive ways to conceptualize our development. He defines each stage of our development as a "crisis." However, "crisis," for him, really just means there are two oppositional forces at each stage of our life. For example, he views the first years of life as the "trust versus mistrust" phase. In short, if an infant's need for love, nutrition and comfort are met, the baby generally learns to trust in the world to meet his needs. His approach to relationships will be one of trust and security. On the other hand, if his needs are unmet, he may strap on a lens of mistrust, which can hamper later developmental stages. Positive resolution of each life stage allows for greater adaption and success in life. The opposite is also true; a negative result in any stage can make subsequent stages in life difficult to successfully navigate.

As my client talked to me about how his adoption had affected his life, I realized how important it is to an adoptive child that there be full disclosure from the beginning. According to Erikson's theories, my client was smack-dab in the midst of the "identity versus isolation" phase of his development. During this stage, a person develops a strong sense of self-identity. When a person is faced with who he thought he was versus who he really is, the clash of identities may produce aberrations of personality. It became impossible for Ron to find security in his identity, which left him feeling isolated—so isolated that the thought of complete isolation in jail was not frightening.

Being alone is hard. Ron felt as though no one understood him and that he owed nothing to anyone. He felt no accountability to his adoptive parents or society as a whole. He had been lied to and deceived, which ultimately left him in a place where he had total apathy toward life.

If you are considering adoption, there is a boatload of research that warns about the detrimental outcomes of deception and lies as a way to cover up the truth of your child's adoption story. Most adoptive parents have received this memo loud and clear and start sharing their child's adoption story with them from toddlerhood. What still varies in the transparency of adoption, however, is whether you choose to have open or closed communication with your child's birth family.

Certain circumstances may dictate a particular direction for your choice, but I will share with you why we decided to seek an open adoption and how we've proceeded with that relationship.

As a psychology instructor, I am kept abreast of recent research, and I often find myself surfing databases of scientific research outcomes to share with my classes. When it came to my adoption questions, I referred to the core of scientific literature to make the decision between open and closed adoption. Of course, my experience as a therapist already swayed me toward an open adoption, but I wanted to verify a few items through research outcomes. Here are a few key outcomes I found in my search for answers.

- "Currently, the vast majority (up to 95%) of adoption agencies which place infants via domestic, private adoption offer options for openness arrangements between birth and adoptive families."[1]

- "Children's reports of greater adoption communicative openness in their families were associated with greater birth family contact, as well as with children's greater self-esteem and fewer behavior problems."[2]
- "While adoptees were more satisfied with contact when there was current birth parent contact," in adoptions where there was no birth parent contact, the researchers found that "adoptees were also more satisfied when communication with their *adoptive* parents was sensitive and open."[3]

What I take from that research is this; 1) most agencies and professionals in adoption are leaning toward open adoption; 2) contact with birth family could lead to better socio-emotional outcomes; 3) and even in situations where there is no birth family contact, it is still possible to make an equally positive impact as an adoptive parent by openly and sensitively communicating with your adoptive child.

For us, given our particular set of circumstances, we felt that an open adoption and contact with our birth family would best enable our child to navigate the truth of adoption.

A common question I receive from acquaintances is, "Aren't you afraid the birth family will take Annika back if you send cute pictures of her?"

I am married to a lawyer and, therefore, I find solace in the law. Once our adoption was finalized, I knew that Annika's life was protected by the clear and comprehensive language of the adoption papers. It is true that one hears about adopted children being sought after by their birth parents in fierce legal battles, and that is why this next point is so critical. Hire the very best lawyer you can find, and follow his/her advice to the letter! Leave no loopholes to be contested later. In our case, fear that continued contact and communication with our birth family might spur on a legal battle was nonexistent.

Our open adoption includes factors that some may be uncomfortable with, but we have found it to be hugely successful and, in the long-term, believe it will be a healthy connection for Annika to have. Before Annika was born, I started a Facebook page for her birth family. I only allow friend requests that are from her birth family and her birth family's friends. Every few weeks, I post pictures for them to see, and I explain what we are up to. To this day, there has been an immediate and loving response to all these posts. I actually keep and print those responses. Her birth father regularly comments on how beautiful she is or how her smile is just like one of her birth-siblings. Her birth grandmother posts, "Tell her I love her, and give her a big hug for me." I am so thrilled Annika will feel their love as she grows up. We are with her every day, but I believe she will feel the love that her birth family has for her. We also send pictures and a letter to her birth mother and father every six months. At Christmas, we send little gifts to her birth family as well as a Christmas card.

Research addresses a few important circumstances to note. If your child was adopted internationally, you may want to consider keeping in touch with the orphanage by corresponding with staff. One sound piece of advice from the research is that if there is a history of mental illness, substance abuse or violence, I recommend that you talk to a social worker and/or counselor to assess the level of risk involved before committing to an open adoption.

Post-adoption contract agreements (PACAs) have become more prevalent in the past few years. This is a written agreement between the birth family and the adoptive family that outlines ongoing contact between the adoptive parents, birthparents, and child in an open adoption. This can include the future frequency of photo exchanges, updates, phone calls, emails, and visits. One point to keep in mind is that these are not always legally enforceable (depends on the state) and a court intervention stemming from a breached PACA would *not* effect the status of the adoption.

In Proverbs 12:22, we are reminded that "The LORD detests lying lips, but he delights in people who are trustworthy." Every adoptive parent wants the very best for the child. We do not want him or her to be hurt with harsh truths, however their stories will have elements of sadness and loss. It is inevitable, and we can't control it. But what we *can* control is how we communicate those truths to our child. Our God wants us to lovingly and considerately establish our child's environment and share a story that is based on truths. Irrespective of whether your child's adoption is open or a closed, your loving and truthful actions and words will communicate the love that will allow your child to thrive. All the while, the Lord will be delighting in your selfless act of adopting one of His.

Scripture

Proverbs 12:22
The LORD detests lying lips, but he delights in people who are trustworthy.

Thoughts Along the Way

Trust is a big consideration as you decide how to proceed with an open adoption. There are varying levels of openness, and those decision points along the way will be dependent upon that level of trust. Do you give your birth family your cell number? What about your address? We are open with our identifying information, but there could be situations where, if the birth family has a history of severe mental illness, interpersonal violence or addictions, you may want to keep your contact information private.

24

DIAL TONE

Normalizing Doubt

Alone in my van, driving to Michael's craft store to purchase some fall decorations, I allowed my mind to wander. I wondered what our child would look like and how it would feel to hold her for the first time. As with a decadent cake that you know you might regret eating later when you step on the scale, I indulged in sweet thoughts of our child-to-be.

I was jolted out of my happy thoughts by the adoption phone. With a pang in my stomach and a beating heart, I blindly dug in my purse and hit the accept button. It was Caroline. Never knowing if her voice would bring an encouraging update or a trouble-shooting dilemma, I held my breath.

I admit that there was a dark space of doubt in the back of my mind in which I considered that she might be calling to rescind on our adoption plan. Her voice seemed troubled, and her speech was frenzied. I tried to piece the fragmented story together, but the bottom line was that their car had broken down, and the cost to fix it would exceed the worth of the car. She wanted to know if we could help them purchase a new car.

I wanted to say, "Absolutely!" But I feared that our lawyer would say, "Absolutely not." I paused, gathered my thoughts and responded honestly.

"I really hope we can help you with this situation. Let me call Mark and run it by him. I am so sorry. I can hear the stress in your voice. Let me see what I can do."

Calls to both Joel and our lawyer confirmed that purchasing a new car was beyond the scope of the laws for adoption in Wisconsin. There could be some wiggle room for a car repair, but that was the extent of the help we could offer.

I felt horrible. Dialing her number, I felt so cheap. Our selfless birth mom was offering life to our family, and I had to deny her plea for help in this situation. How could I mince words to make this sound okay? I had to simply chop away; there was no way of getting around the truth.

I expressed to her my regret. "We cannot pay for a new car," followed by my dribble of reasoning, including the state laws that bind us to certain rules and regulations with the adoption. There was silence. Then more silence.

"Hello?"

I am not sure at what point Caroline hung up on me, but it was probably right after the words "We cannot..." In my optimistic mind, I considered that perhaps we simply got cut off, perhaps she lost cell reception. I called her number, but there was no answer. I knew I should not have eaten that stupid piece of "What's it going to be like to hold my baby" cake.

I didn't know what her hang up meant. Was she just upset, or was she backing out? I made a call to our social worker in Wisconsin. She was my eyes and ears in the community since we lived many states away. After telling her what happened, she assured me that she would follow up with Caroline to assess the situation.

Two days passed, and finally we got word back from Vivian, our social worker. She had made contact with our birth mom and shared that Caroline felt terribly bad about hanging up; she was just really emotional in that moment. That car was her and Michael's sole transportation and, without it, they could not work or go to the doctor. While her response was understandable, the small voice of doubt was finding fertile soil in which to grow.

Doubt is inevitable. Doubt is defined as "to be uncertain about" or "to be afraid of." Think of all the big decisions you've ever made: getting married, buying a house, selling a house, moving, finding a job, accepting a job, purchasing a car. Some (or all) of these experiences may have elicited an element of uncertainty or fear. Adoption is no different. Doubt is normal. It is expected that one may doubt a birth mother's ability to follow through with her commitment to an adoption plan. It is normal for your birth mother to doubt her own strength and decision to adopt.

As a counselor, I attempt to normalize my clients' negative feelings to an aversive situation. What mother would not be irate that her child is sneaking out in the middle of the night, and what teen would not be dizzy with frustration dealing with an overprotective mother who will not give an ounce of freedom to her maturing daughter? It's not that either is right or wrong; both mother and daughter have strong feelings that are justified.

Let me give you an example of how I normalized doubt with our birth mom. Sleeping soundly, I was jolted awake by the sound of the adoption phone. I looked at my clock: it was 2:02 a.m., which wasn't a good sign. Even considering the time change between Wisconsin and Maryland, it was still quite late.

I answered. "Hello, Caroline what's up? Are you okay?"

She was crying. She expressed concern that we would not communicate or send pictures once we adopted. My goal in this conversation was twofold. First, I wanted to assure her that we were committed to this baby knowing her birth family as well as to our continued communication about her growth and accomplishments all along the way. Second, I wanted her to know that fear and uncertainty is normal. I genuinely stated, "This is such an important decision that if you did not consider those things, it would be abnormal." I encouraged her to talk with me, to talk about those fears and concerns so that we could work through them together. I reminded her, "I see us as a team, coming together in the Lord's larger plan for this baby. We need to plod through the doubt together."

If you can trek through the smaller "freak-out" moments together before the birth, normalizing them as part of the adoption process, you start to build confidence that you can make it through the big day, birth day.

Backup a few thousand years. Even the disciples had doubt! Jesus had clearly communicated what to expect after his death. He told his disciples that he would die and rise again on the third day. They listened intently to Jesus. Yet Luke 24:37-39 sheds light on their doubt. "They were startled and frightened, thinking they saw a ghost. He said to them, 'Why are you troubled, and why do doubts rise in your minds? Look at my hands and my feet. It is I myself! Touch me and see; a ghost does not have flesh and bones, as you see I have.'"

When he said this, he showed them his hands and feet. The Lord's most trusted and devout followers doubted his word. Doubt is normal. It is human. What did the Lord do in response to their doubt? "He showed them his hands and feet," with holes as powerful reminders of his crucifixion.

Throughout our adoption, I had to stay focused on the hands and feet of Christ. The Lord revealed himself to me on the old country road, called us to adopt and then began clearing this amazing path to our child. No matter what your adoption story is, it is critical to stay focused on those tangible signs that the Lord provides you in order to ease those feelings of doubt.

Doubt is born of uncertainty, but also of fear. Beth Moore sheds instructive light on fear. She states a profound truth, "It's tough being a woman in the tight fist of fear."[1] Then she wraps us up in the warm blanket of God's love and reminds us that, "Every time you're in a tight fist of fear, remember you're in something much tighter. God is holding you in the palm of his hand. Isaiah 49:16 says, "See, I have engraved you on the palms of my hands.""

It is powerful to think that God has got you in the palm of His hand. There were times during our adoption that I envisioned myself literally being held by the Lord. Talk about a sense of calm.

You will, as we did, bump along the chaotic adoption path, wrought with inevitable doubt. But the faith that you have in our Lord will trump the doubt. You will hear His voice and see His work in the midst of this process. I trust that at the end of the journey you will end up with a baby snuggled in your arms, your lips praising God's goodness.

Scripture

Luke 24:37-39
They were startled and frightened, thinking they saw a ghost. He said to them, "Why are you troubled, and why do doubts rise in your minds? Look at my hands and my feet. It is I myself! Touch me and see; a ghost does not have flesh and bones, as you see I have."

Isaiah 49:16
See I have engraved you on the palm of my hands.

Thoughts Along the Way

What is your deepest fear when it comes to adoption? Close your eyes, picture yourself being held in the palm of the Lord's hand. Now exhale, and rest secure in his promises.

If you want a fabulous bible study during your adoption journey, look to Beth Moore's study, *Esther: It's Tough Being A Woman*. This quote from her study has stuck with me: "But trust reverses the detours of adversity into highways of destiny."[1]

25

NAIVETY

The Lord's Plan Being Revealed

Joel and I lounged on the couch, recuperating from the craziness of Christmas and New Year's festivities. The night before we had a fierce Wii *Just Dance* competition with our treasured friends, Lisa and Eric Beers and their two children. We had been stationed together with the Beers twice before in Texas and Hawaii. Then in the midst of our adoption journey, the Lord intervened in the military assignment process, and brought them to Maryland just down the street from us. Talk about a gracious and loving God. He simply delivered one of my best friends to my doorstep. That night brought much needed stress relief as the eight of us battled it out, laughing at each others ridiculous dance moves!

That next evening, like two blobs, we meshed, spooned together while watching a mindless show. It was late, around 10:00p.m., when the adoption phone rang. I jumped up, adrenaline pushing me back into the land of the living. Caroline's voice came between heavy breaths. She was having contractions and was at the hospital. Our baby was going to make an early entry into this world.

My mind whirled as I hung up. Joel could see by my expression that the time had come for action. While we had prepared the baby's room and made a few preliminary arrangements, the news from Wisconsin still caught us by surprise. Alex and Kelsey had been asleep but were now at the top of the stairs demanding to know the cause of our excitement. I heard Joel's voice explaining as he packed our suitcase. I hollered for them to pack a few things for an overnight stay. We dashed through the house, literally barking out orders as we darted past one another in the hall. A call to my friend Lisa secured us childcare. Another call to Joel's parents in Arizona prompted a frantic booking of a flight to arrive late the next day. I knew their presence would usher in a sense of normalcy for our children (and also a lot of Grandma's chocolate chip cookies).

After a quick Web browse, two airline tickets were purchased for the early flight out of Baltimore, Maryland. We quickly gathered our adoption papers and placed them in a binder. Joel made an emergency call to his boss at work and explained our situation. We prayed that our baby would not be born until we arrived.

Running on no sleep, in the dark of early morning, Joel pushed a luggage cart overflowing with suitcases, diaper bags, a playpen and an infant car seat through the deserted terminal. The two of us strode in together, praying that the next time we were in this terminal it would be with our new daughter.

I received another call from Caroline while we were going through security. The contractions were coming more frequently. The news only brought on more stress. We were just hours away.

Hang-on, I prayed.

The TSA agent at the airport seemed to be in no hurry. He looked us up and down and then examined our identification cards and tickets. I smiled as if all were normal, but my insides twisted and turned. I did not want to miss our daughter's birth!

Joel pushed the empty stroller to the gate, and as we waited in line on the jet way one of the baggage handlers looked suspiciously at the stroller with no baby. Since we were merely standing around, I took the time to explain to her that we were adopting and in a hurry to get to the hospital, as our baby was about to be born. She was so sweet and gave us assurances of a timely departure. Grabbing her walkie-talkie, she gruffly barked, "We've got a couple adopting. Baby is about to be born. On-time takeoff a priority." My heart calmed. Others were pulling for us. Our parents and friends were praying for us, and we felt those prayers. Seated and buckled in, the announcement was made to turn off all electronic devices for departure. Oh, how I hoped that in two hours when I turned that phone back on there would not be a text stating, "Annika has arrived."

As we approached Milwaukee, the sun broke through billowy, white clouds. With a Great Lake beneath and a great light from the Lord above, I heard Him whisper, "I've got this." I felt God's presence, His calming spirit, penetrate my tense body. Don't get me wrong, I was on a mission to get to that hospital on time, but I was no longer in a frenzied panic. We touched down, and there was no text. Just one more leg to this journey: the drive.

My husband knew to let me handle the rental car. Joel is way too nice, and would need me to cut short the usual offers from the rental car representative. My voice was stern.

"We would like a car, no extra insurance or upgrades."

Of course, our rental car employee explained that it was his first day on the job. I then calmly but firmly stated that time was of the essence as our baby was about to be born. He wanted to complete the 30-point inspection of the car prior to us leaving, which included how to place the key in the ignition to turn on the car. Seriously? I needed to be firmer.

"We need to leave now. Give me the keys."

We exited the terminal to find that, in the dead of a Wisconsin winter, there was no snow on the ground. The Lord had cleared the way for us. Just two hours more and we would be pulling into the hospital. Joel drove, pushing the speed limit but being mindful of the need for safety. The pressure to get there mounted as he pressed his foot on the gas pedal. Our car ride together was eerily quiet, as each of us counted the minutes ticking by. After sixteen years of marriage, even in our silence we could harmonize our anxiety.

I called Caroline to let her know that we would be there in just a few hours. She told us that a decision had been made to break her water, but they would wait until we arrived. Perfect!

Pulling into the parking lot, I quickly grabbed the big teddy bear (one of our adoption gifts for Caroline), Joel threw a diaper bag over his shoulder and we rushed through the double doors of the entrance. Here we were, walking into the hospital where our child would be born. How the next few hours and days would play out was unimaginable.

The small-town community hospital greeted us with warmth, but it was not well versed in adoption. Not sure where to put us, they huddled in the nurses station trying to figure out a plan. They finally explained that they would put us in a room down the hall from Caroline. The nurse was kind but completely caught off guard by our adoption plan.

I explained, "Caroline would like for us to be in the room when Annika is delivered." She nodded, but you could see a look of suspicion in her eyes. My look of determination, however, out-matched the nurse's doubts.

We dropped our things and were ushered to the birthing room. As we entered, big smiles came over all our faces. Caroline was relieved that we had made it, and we were beyond thrilled that she was relieved. We could hear Annika's monitored heartbeat. She was alive and about to be delivered into this world to four beings that loved her with all their hearts.

Internally, I did a happy dance, thinking of all the people involved in Annika's story. She would be completely naive to the preparations that had been made for her arrival. She did not know how the Lord had been working many years before her arrival to put an amazing plan in place for her life. She was oblivious to what tremendous care and labor had gone into preparing for the arrival. She would be born naive to the blessings the Lord had already bestowed upon her. But, in time, she would hear her story and learn of the mighty Lord's plan for her life, and her faith would be made stronger because of it.

I suspect that this is the same way the Lord often sees me. He's planning, working and executing blessings of a master plan, but I am—most times—completely ignorant to His elaborate plan.

In Psalm 139:13-16, the psalmist sings praises to the Lord:

> For you created my inmost being;
> you knit me together in my mother's womb.
> praise you because I am fearfully and wonderfully made;
> your works are wonderful,
> I know that full well.
> My frame was not hidden from you
> when I was made in the secret place,
> when I was woven together in the depths of the earth.
> Your eyes saw my unformed body;
> all the days ordained for me were written in your book
> before one of them came to be.

In that moment, listening to the whooshes emanating from the ultrasound monitor, my baby in another woman's womb, I was struck like this psalmist. The Lord had been planning for this child before her creation. His call to me on that old country road was a call for me to be the mother of a child he had plans to create five years later. He loved Annika even before she was created.

"Your eyes saw my unformed body; all the days ordained for me were written in your book before one of them came to be." How do you even begin to conceptualize the depths of the Lord's love for us when he can love you even before your creation? It simply blows my mind!

Scripture

Psalm 139:13-16
For you created my inmost being;
you knit me together in my mother's womb.
I praise you because I am fearfully and wonderfully made;
your works are wonderful,
I know that full well.
My frame was not hidden from you
when I was made in the secret place,
when I was woven together in the depths of the earth.
Your eyes saw my unformed body;
all the days ordained for me were written in your book
before one of them came to be.

Thoughts Along the Way

Have you ever stopped to ponder that God was saying your name before He created the universe? Think about that. Relish it. You are exactly where you are supposed to be, doing what He intended for you to do.

26

IN THE BIRTHING ROOM

Impossibility of Reciprocity

I've always had a hard time explaining the moment that Annika was handed to us. We traveled to Wisconsin pushing an empty stroller, and that very same afternoon, we were given a precious life. The place where there was a void in the morning was completely full that afternoon. Life changed dramatically that day.

Shortly after we arrived at the hospital, the doctor broke Caroline's water and advised us that it would probably be an hour or so before pushing began. Joel and I were running on adrenaline. A bathroom break and a bit of food seemed like a wise idea. We were so excited that eating seemed impossible—but necessary. We had pie and milk to calm our nerves. A text on Joel's phone advised us it was time; Caroline was ready to deliver.

We downed our milk and ran to the elevator. I jabbed the up button. It glowed white and remained so. "Ding!" We hurriedly stepped in, and I repeatedly stabbed the "close door" button. We both took a deep breath as we entered the birthing room, manned by experts who went about their work with little conversation. Caroline was sweaty as she endured the pain of childbirth. Having labored myself twice, I knew her pain. I felt guilty that I was not the one suffering.

Joel was behind me as I moved along one side of the bed. Michael was on the other side, holding Caroline's hand. Joel moved close to me, looking over my shoulder. The nurses encouraged Caroline to push and for Michael and me to help the process by holding up Caroline's legs. We were in the thick of it; Team Annika was in full action.

After just a few pushes, a little head came forth, followed quickly by shoulders and a precious little body. She was born. Annika Lynn-Marie England was born. With umbilical cord still attached, Caroline held Annika for a moment. Then the nurses wiped and assessed. Everything moved so quickly, yet in slow motion, while I waited for my turn to hold my baby. Finally, the nurses had done their required interventions, and they smiled and extended their arms, and Annika was handed to me. With Joel by my side we stared in adoring silence at this tiny child. Tears blurred my view of her perfect face. Maybe it was one minute, maybe it was five—time stopped with her in my arms. Somehow, my brain finally won over my heart, and I became aware of others in the room. I wanted Joel and Michael to also hold Annika. Selfishly, I did not want to let go, but I forced myself to do so. Michael, our tall and sensitive birth father, gently held her and smiled down at this innocent life he had helped create. His inherent love for her was evident. Selfless is truly the best word to describe what might have been one of the hardest days for our birth mother and father.

Then Joel cradled Annika in his arms. After gazing into the wide eyes of his newborn daughter, he looked up for a moment. Joel and Caroline made eye contact, and instinctively Joel said, "Thank you." He truly meant those words, but was struck with how insufficient the statement was. He said it anyway, realizing that no words would be enough to communicate his gratitude.

I've tried to describe to others the feeling of being handed the life of a child. It's entirely humbling, joyful and awkward all at the same time. I believe this unavoidable paradox of feelings is at least partly understood through the lens of a concept in psychology called reciprocity.

Research in psychology demonstrates that humans have a tendency to want to reciprocate kindness. A neighbor brings you banana bread, and you feel obligated to return that kindness with a batch of cookies. Even the smallest token of kindness stirs our human nature to respond with an equivalent gesture. As one increases the value of a gift, the more one feels a need to give back. Let's up the ante. Imagine if a stranger approached you on the street and handed you a two-karat diamond ring as a gift, with no strings attached. And that diamond ring was actually their family heirloom. What would you say? How would you feel? How much more would you feel in debt to repay someone who gave you a diamond ring? Would you hug them? Say thank you a million times? Jump up and down?

Every joyful moment of our time in the delivery room was seared in my memory, but I could not ignore the heaviness on my heart that we were being given something that we could never repay. The weight of the loss and grief that our birth family faced when surrendering this child to us was difficult to bear. My heart was completely filled and simultaneously broken.

Just as Annika was a sacrificial gift, so is our eternal salvation. We did nothing to earn Annika. She was a gift of love that we can never repay. Likewise, we can do nothing to earn our eternal salvation. It is by grace that we are saved. When I think of Christ's death on the cross, I wonder who can fully understand such a gift? In Ephesians 2:8 it states, "For it is by grace you have been saved, through faith—and this is not from yourselves, it is the gift of God." I want to emphasize that your child is not something you can *earn.*

I know, at this point, it is completely understandable to feel as though you've earned *something*, after all the paperwork, the hoops you've jumped through, the stress you've (barely) managed. I hear a defeated sigh through the pages. But in the moment in which your birth mom makes the decision to hand a bundle of life into your arms, you are struck by the monumental nature of the gift you are receiving. Make no mistake, her sacrifice of love for this child is much larger and more significant than the mountain of paperwork and sleepless nights you have endured. If we zoom even further out from the birth room, you can see that this child was planned for well before you even considered adoption. You, this child and your birth mom were all a part of God's master plan from the time of creation. Now, take that lens and zoom it all the way out, for an eternal perspective. You, God's child, are so precious in His eyes that he was willing to sacrifice His only son for your eternal salvation. Soak up that truth!

The fact is that there is nothing you did to earn this child; it is by grace alone that you have been blessed with this life and it is by grace alone that you have eternal salvation in Christ Jesus.

Take the pressure off yourself about what you will say or how you should react when you receive your child, or laboring over just the right birth mother gift to bring. The Lord has brought you to this point, and regardless of the outcome, He will lift you up and carry you through this time. Gratitude in the face of grace is all that is required.

Scripture

Ephesians 2:8
For it is by grace you have been saved, through faith—and this is not from yourselves, it is the gift of God.

Thoughts Along the Way

Be you; be in the moment. Accept this amazing gift with humility and awestruck wonder. Enjoy. Enjoy. Enjoy.

If you are intrigued by the truth, "it is by grace alone that you have eternal salvation in Christ Jesus," and want to learn more, I recommend *Basic Christianity* by John Stott.[1] Whether you are a seeker or a skeptic, this book will elaborate and the core truths of Christianity that we discover through the adoption process.

27

23 STEPS AWAY

Choosing Love

Joel and I, cradling newborn Annika, walked 23 steps down the hallway to our own room, allowing us not only physical space but also emotional space from our birth family. We permitted our joy to release unabated. In the delivery room, we felt torn between our elation and the empathetic sadness we felt for Caroline, Michael and Julia. But in the privacy of our own room and in the quiet of our own hearts, the trumpets were joyously sounding. Holding Annika in his arms, Joel's wall of cautious emotion, came crumbling down as tears of joy streamed down his cheeks.

Thrill and celebration were to be expected, but something quite unexpected happened also. That day, we *chose* to love Annika. When Kelsey and Alex were born, we knew they were ours. There was no question as to who would raise them. However, for the next 30 days, in accordance with Wisconsin law, Annika technically belonged to Caroline and Michael. Sure, we had Caroline's assurances that she wanted us to raise Annika and be her parents, but the law did not fully award us those rights until the Termination of Parental Rights hearing. She was in our arms, but she was not legally ours.

In that hushed hospital room on our daughter's birthday, we both whispered into her precious ear three words that opened the floodgates to our hearts: "I love you." Whether she was to be ours for our eternal existence or just for an hour or for 30 days, we were committed to this little one. Up until that point, the risk of connecting to a birth mom and financially investing in adoption had limited emotional consequence if met with a change of mind. But now, it would mean complete and total heartache. So we *chose* that day to accept the potential emotional wreckage of an adoption failure and moved forward with Annika as ours—just not yet legally ours.

In the entirety of our marriage, this first week with Annika might stand as one of the most cherished memories of our 20 years together. Vulnerable and faithful, comforting and loving, Joel stood as a pillar of strength for me. This journey led us to a place of complete unknown, and our reliance upon each other was absolute. Exhausted, excited and scared we journeyed through the first few days of Annika's life together. Being united in our approach was suddenly more relevant than ever. The crisp reality of Annika's cold winter birth was that Joel and I *needed* each other. Overwhelmed, I was drowning in both love and uncertainty, and it was in his arms where I found my breath of peace.

Joel is not only an incredible husband, he also loves babies. In all honesty, he is much better with infants than I am. He inherited this incredible gift from his father. Both the England men have a chest labeled *Infant Sleep Zone*. With unlimited patience, a warm smile and a soft, reassuring voice, he can easily bounce and sway a baby to contentment, and the joy in his heart while doing so is pure. Consequently, in the midst of my sleep deprivation, that is the sexiest characteristic any man can have.

Our two-day hospital stay was punctuated by the typical nurse visits, first shots for Annika and a lesson in bottle-feeding. We also had many of Annika's birth family members who came to see Caroline and spend some time with Annika. While we wanted Caroline, Michael, Julia and other family members to see and hold Annika, it was admittedly terrifying. Would one stare, one emotional moment or Annika's innocent cry tip the scales and have them running for the door with her in their arms? But we trusted that there was a higher plan and that all the human rationale that makes a change of mind plausible was really impossible because this was the Lord's doing. We gave them their space to grieve, and part of that grieving is acknowledging the monumental loss of being an active parent or grandparent to this child. The morning after Annika was born, Caroline was discharged. She left the hospital with her own family while we stayed behind with our infant daughter.

I would find out years later that this was the most difficult point in the adoption for our birth family. One can only imagine the heartbreak of leaving the hospital empty-handed. Julia shared with me, "What got us through was picturing you and Joel holding Annika walking out of the hospital. We knew it was the right thing, but it was hard."

Now that our baby was in our arms, there was nothing as terrifying as the thought of our birth mother changing her mind. We went to Wisconsin with a good deal of anxiety in our hearts, partly because this possibility lingered in the back of our minds. It is likely that nothing an adoptive parent reads or hears will totally dissolve that sense of anxiety. The fact is that a birth mother can change her mind up until parental rights are terminated (the wait time varies from state to state). But it is rare. One of the best articles on this comes from the Family Education website. These statistics calmed my fears:

> "One agency said, 'In 10 years, in 4 of 940 placements have children been returned to birthparents.' Another said, 'Of approximately 700 placements, there have been approximately 10 such cases.' Of the attorneys who responded to the question, I received such comments as 'In over 1,000 adoptions, only 5 fall-throughs *after* the placement was made.'"[1]

Moving forward from that first "I love you," I was Annika's mom, and Joel was her dad. This was clearly demonstrated when a nurse came in to give Annika her first bath. She proceeded to wash Annika's plentiful black hair, scrubbing to get the blood out of her curly locks, and as Annika began to cry, I quickly intervened. In my head, I gave that cold, mean nurse the name "Bull," and I firmly requested that she be gentler with my baby. Occasionally, people will ask me, "Is there a difference between raising Annika and your biological children?" My answer is, "No." My love for her is just as deep, my protection of her equally fierce and my dedication to her needs, unequivocal.

If I could choose one word to describe those first few days after Annika was born, it would be overwhelmed. I was simply emotionally overrun with joy, love and fear. There was a moment during that first week when I pried myself away from Annika for 20 minutes to take a walk. I needed to pause to pray and worship. I borrowed Joel's phone because my phone battery was depleted from all the pictures I had taken. Subjected to his less-than-stellar selection of worship music, I pressed on. And then a song I've heard many times before, but never connected with or related to, piped in through the headphones. Mercy Me's "Word of God Speak" played to my heart:

Word of God speak
Would You pour down like rain
Washing my eyes to see
Your majesty

To be still and know
That You're in this place
Please let me stay and rest
In Your holiness
Word of God speak

Just for a moment, I needed to be that child, lying on my Father's chest. Even when I tried to pray, I could not find the words I wanted to speak. Oh how I wanted to shout the Lord's majesty. Yet I was temporarily frozen by emotional overload. When I heard that song, I was reminded that the Lord knew my needs, my heart and my joy. He didn't need me to shout it from a mountaintop; He was hearing it loud and clear from the depths of my soul. I could take rest in His presence and feel the calm from His word. In Romans 8:26, the role of the Holy Spirit is explained. It says, "We do not know what we ought to pray for, but the Spirit himself intercedes for us through wordless groans." Whether your emotional overload is joy or grief, when words are absent you can pass that load on to the Holy Spirit and it will be communicated with perfection. Oh thank goodness for that!

Scripture

Romans 8:26
We do not know what we ought to pray for, but the Spirit himself intercedes for us through wordless groans.

Thoughts Along the Way

Maybe you wrote down a birth plan. Perhaps you have a suitcase for the baby filled with onesies and diapers. What you cannot pack so neatly is the way your heart will feel once God's plan is revealed. Take time *now* to thank God in advance for what He is about to do. And do not be surprised if you are speechless in the presence of the Lord's glory.

28

THE FARM

Being Cared For

After three days in the hospital, Annika was discharged. Joel carried her in his arms as I led the way. The eyes of those seated in the waiting area followed our exiting steps. Those quiet observers, waiting for their name to be called by the nurse in white, saw the typical family with a strong husband leaving the hospital, carrying his newborn in one hand and opening the door for his diaper-bag toting wife. Yet the latent, underlying truth of that moment was that this exit was the culmination of a higher plan. Our steps all along this journey were propelled by faith, and those bystanders were witnessing a promise upheld by the Lord.

What we wanted to do at that point was board the first plane back to Maryland, unite Annika with her sister and brother and begin our life as a family of five. What we *needed* to do was stay put in Wisconsin. The best we could do was to call home and spend some time talking to Kelsey and Alex. Joel's parents were there, and they were a stable foundation for our kids when it was most needed. Still, we took the time each night to let each child talk through his or her school day. We explained to our children what was happening and why it was taking so long.

There were a few factors that delayed our return home. First, we wanted to provide our birth family with an opportunity to visit with Annika outside the sterile and emotionally charged hospital. We also wanted to ensure that Annika went to her first doctor's appointment within five days of discharge, which was a critical piece of the adoption in terms of paperwork. Finally, there were two legal factors that played a part in our decision-making. Wisconsin requires approximately 30 days to acquire a court date for the Termination of Parental Rights hearing. Since Annika was not legally our child, we had to obtain permission from both Wisconsin and Maryland to take Annika across state lines. It is called the Interstate Compact on the Placement of Children (ICPC) law, and all out-of-state adopting parents have to jump through this legal hoop in order to return home with their adopted child if the Termination of Parental Rights hearing is not yet complete. For us, completing this legal paperwork took about two weeks.

Joel and I made a short drive from the exit of the hospital just across the street to a Holiday Inn, where we stayed for five days. We made friends with the local waitress at the hotel restaurant, and chatted frequently with the desk clerk. We learned that while cheese curds sound disgusting, they taste amazing. The Holiday Inn staff came to know our story, and we came to appreciate their kind support and inquisitive nature. Without family there, it was nice to share our unfolding story with others.

Our decision to encourage birth family visits with Annika was met with skepticism from our nervous family and friends. But, as a counselor who understands the process of grief, I know that loss necessitates time for closure. Seeing, holding and saying goodbye was something I knew her birth family had to do so that they were not left with questions. I will not kid you; during each visit Joel and I were definitely on pins and needles. We prayed before, we prayed during, we prayed after. It was hard. Within the confines of a small hotel room, we all "ooohed" and "ahhhed" at tiny Annika. Caroline and her mom looked at her precious face and commented on whose features she had. They compared her skin and hair to those of her biological siblings. They took it all in, and so did we. We were able to take pictures together, which now sit framed in Annika's room. Michael also visited, and while holding Annika his facial expression was simultaneously one of great joy and great loss. For all who visited, tears were shed and loss was deep. Our birth family's courage to seek closure by saying goodbye was a testament to their incredible strength. Once everyone had a chance to visit, though, and the doctor's visit was complete, we felt a need to focus on our family in a more removed location.

DJ, one of Joel's closest friends from college, grew up in Wisconsin. His parents live on a vast and gorgeous farm in the southern part of the state. In late January, the Wisconsin countryside was frozen and lifeless. As we walked into their inviting home, the entire living room with its one large glass window felt connected to the rolling pastures and grazing horse and cattle behind the house.

Dave and Ida Walsh, DJ's parents and his uncle welcomed us as family, showing us to our room in the completely renovated bed-and-breakfast style basement, adorned with Americana decorative signs and a homemade quilt on the bed. We immediately felt at home.

After a few days during which we unwound from the drama-filled events of Annika's birth, we made some important decisions. The quietness of the farm allowed us to think clearly, and we concluded that the best course of action was for Joel to stay on the farm for just a few days and then return home to Kelsey and Alex. I would remain at the farm until we were given our lawyer's "all clear" for Annika's travel across state lines. We also decided not to attend the Termination of Parental Rights hearing, as staying in Wisconsin for the full 30 days in order to attend seemed too long to be away from Kelsey and Alex. Instead, we created a plan to have our social worker and lawyer work on our behalf to ensure Caroline and Michael's presence at that hearing.

With course direction in place, it was time to relax with my baby in my arms. One day, I sleepily crept up the basement stairs to feed Annika just at the break of morning. I cradled my newborn as shafts of winter morning sunlight streaked across the room. They illuminated Annika's soft face. Then the sunlight turned to gray, and snow began falling in silent, leafy flakes that evaporated when they touched the ground. In the warm kitchen, I, too, felt cradled and thanked the Lord for this place of serenity to which He had led us.

The Walshes were my stand-in family for those special first weeks with Annika. My appreciation for their generous hospitality is lifelong. We drank coffee together in the morning and ate delicious home-cooked meals. I remained strong in my confidence that the Lord's plan was fully in place, but my steadfast faith was not without emotion. There were a few moments in my time at the farm in which I was overwhelmed. Good tears. Big, no-holding-back tears.

For both Joel and I, our hands-down favorite moments were the quiet, hushed naps with Annika on one of our chests, singing lullabies to our new daughter. Seared in my memory is one such lullaby. In the midst of singing Brahms Lullaby, I was overtaken by a feeling I had never before felt. For 38 years, I had sung praise songs, hymns, prayed aloud and cried to the Lord at times, but never from a place so deep within. That day, I felt what it was like to sing from my soul. It was that afternoon, with Annika resting her ear to my heart, that I fully understood what soul is. After I stopped singing, I sat in silence and cherished that feeling of my soul on fire, warming me to the core. My tears came from a place of pure gratitude for this child, the deep love I felt for her, and the Lord's faithful deliverance of his promise.

A few days after Joel returned to Maryland, Dave and Ida invited me to dinner at a local diner to experience a traditional fish fry. In Wisconsin, Fridays are for fish fry. Dave led the way from the car as I pulled Annika's blanket over her face to protect her from the cold. A bell tied to the front door rang as we entered, and a flood of salutations followed. Having grown up in anonymity in a big city in Southern California, the genuine friendships these townspeople had formed were extraordinary. Once seated with drinks ordered, DJ's dad, Dave, motioned for me to go to the buffet where fried cod, cabbage, rolls and a number of delicious desserts awaited. Seated once again and ready to devour this hometown meal, a friend of the Walsh family came over to our table.

Dave graciously introduced me and then, as plain as the white bread and butter on my plate, extended his hand to the infant car seat placed beside me and stated, "...and this is her daughter, Annika." It was the first time anyone had said it out loud—that Annika was my daughter. It hit me like a tidal wave. The tears rolling down my face were unstoppable. I couldn't even pause to explain my rush of emotion. I felt badly for Ida and Dave; I was making a horrible first impression as the sobbing houseguest!

Perhaps the Walsh family acted as the Lord's angels who came to give us comfort when we were emotionally drained. The story in the Bible about Elijah, the prophet, has similarities. At one point, Elijah was exhausted and emotionally overwhelmed:

> "Then he lay down under the bush and fell asleep.
>
> All at once an angel touched him and said, Get up and eat.' He looked around, and there by his head was some bread baked over hot coals, and a jar of water. He ate and drank and then lay down again.
>
> The angel of the LORD came back a second time and touched him and said, 'Get up and eat, for the journey is too much for you.' So he got up and ate and drank. Strengthened by that food, he traveled forty days and forty nights." (1Kings 19:5-9)

Not only did God clear the way for Annika's adoption, he also attended to Joel's and my needs. Welcoming a newborn baby while being far from home, with a Termination of Parental Rights hearing lingering in the distant future, created elements of stress for sure. But through these trying times came moments with Annika that were shared with Joel, and those moments brought the three of us together as nothing else could. There was a long journey ahead; finalization was still six months away. God provided for our strength and sanity. What an awesome God we have!

Scripture

1 Kings 19:5-9
Then he lay down under the bush and fell asleep. All at once an angel touched him and said, 'Get up and eat.' He looked around, and there by his head was some bread baked over hot coals, and a jar of water. He ate and drank and then lay down again. The angel of the LORD came back a second time and touched him and said, 'Get up and eat, for the journey is too much for you.' So he got up and ate and drank. Strengthened by that food, he traveled forty days and forty nights.

Thoughts Along the Way

Just as important as it is to pack a diaper bag, what are the considerations you are making for your own well being and nourishment for post-baby or post-adoption? Who are those supports that will build you up and give you the fuel you need for the road ahead? Be prepared for the Lord to place some angels in your life, and recognize it when it happens. Hallelujah for that!

29

FAMILY OF FIVE

Termination of Parental Rights Hearing

Joel and I made the decision to bring Annika home to Kelsey and Alex, in Maryland, before she was legally ours. That decision was based on faith that the remaining legal details would be resolved on schedule, but I hoped I was not jumping the gun. As soon as the Interstate Compact was approved, I was on the plane from Milwaukee to Baltimore. I knew the moment Kelsey and Alex laid eyes on their sister, she would be just that—their sister. Thus, it created an emotional risk of heartache, since there was that slim—but real—possibility that Caroline or Michael could change their mind. We had 12 more days before the February 1st court date.

I thanked my generous hosts on the farm. Words could never express how much I valued their kindness. The next morning, I was out of bed, gathering my belongings and putting into order what Annika would need for the flight home. I threw the bags into the back seat and secured the infant carrier into the car seat base. I set the car heater on high, as the temperature outside registered -17 degrees.

Annika slept comfortably against my chest in the baby carrier all the way home. From take off until landing, each minute felt like an hour and each hour an eternity. It's like the last mile of a 10K race, when you can see the finish line.

I imagined Kelsey, Alex and Joel waiting in the baggage area at Baltimore Washington airport. Jumping out of their skin to see, touch and love on Annika, they probably watched the empty baggage belts loop around endlessly as they nervously checked the big board for the status of arriving flights.

I exited the plane pushing an empty stroller since Annika was still bundled in the front-pack carrier strapped to my chest. I strode past the security gates and scoured the waiting crowd.

Kelsey and Alex ran to me. Smiles and awe shone from their faces as they soaked up their first glimpse of their sister. I carefully scooped up sleeping Annika from the carrier and sat on an empty bench in the terminal for Kelsey and Alex to each hold her for the first time. Kisses and tears showered her tiny forehead. Their faces were so close to Annika's that they must have triggered her hunger. Her face contorted, and she screamed for her bottle, for comfort and for less chaos around her. I dug into my carry-on and retrieved a bottle of formula. Annika kept up her cry, and I reassured Kelsey and Alex that she was just hungry, not sad. With her stomach full, Annika quieted, and I took a deep breath, sliding down into the seat. Most of the passengers had gone as we gathered up to depart the terminal.

Just like that, after years of thinking, planning, praying, working and contemplating adopting a baby, our family of five fell into step and made our way home.

The hardest part of those first few weeks with our children was playing referee with Kelsey and Alex for "hold time." One morning before school, Alex was pouting.

"Kelsey got to hold Annika for 14 minutes, and I only got 12 minutes."

The morning of the Termination of Parental Rights hearing, I painted a poster. In bright red paint I scripted "Gotcha Day-February 1, 2012." Every letter I painted on that poster was by faith. At noon Wisconsin time, our birth mother and father would have to appear in court and agree to give up their parental rights to Annika.

I trusted this to happen, because I believed in the Lord's plan. But that did not change the fact that the morning went by as slow as molasses in winter. I could not even ponder a picture other than that of Annika becoming ours that day; the alternative was pure heartbreak. Joel and I waited for a phone call on the same couch on which we sat when I first told Joel about my calling on the old country road, the same couch on which we got the call from Caroline that she was in labor.

Finally it came, a ring and quick answer. Holding the phone between our ears, Joel and I received the golden news. Our social worker, Vivian, announced, "Annika is officially yours." And with wobbly legs and beating hearts, Joel and I thankfully stepped off the adoption roller coaster. We smiled, content and relieved, and kissed. My mom was present to witness this life-changing day, and she took pictures and celebrated with us. Kelsey and Alex received a bouquet of balloons upon their exit from school to announce the great news.

Then, the celebrations began. First, ice cream for Kelsey and Alex, then a Gotcha Day party with friends and neighbors. We served Wisconsin cheese, soup and beer!

The month following Annika's adoption, I felt light. The intensity of a calling is something to be reckoned with. It had been over five years that I had lived everyday with the Lord's voice directing me, pushing me, pulling me toward Annika. Now she was in my arms, and there was such relief it was palpable. Yet, at the same time, I missed the Lord's constant tugging at my heart. I was so busy with feeding, diapering and mothering that my normal quiet time with the Lord was nonexistent. I felt guilty that I was not spending more time in prayer, thanking the One who had made our family complete. One cold winter evening after Joel came home, I bundled up and pried myself away for a short run around our neighborhood. With my headphones on, I recentered my thoughts on the Lord. A song that I had originally put on my playlist to remind me of the difficulties that Caroline was facing, "Better Than a Hallelujah" by Amy Grant, streamed through my headphones:

"God loves a lullaby
In a mother's tears in the dead of night
Better than a Hallelujah sometimes"

Through that song, I found the Lord releasing the guilt I had been feeling. He acknowledged the hard job of being a mom to an infant and the reality of my overcrowded day. He gave me the silent pat on the back that I needed. Lyrics streamed in, and tears streamed down my face. I love it when the Lord shows up through a song.

His reaffirming hand on my shoulder during that run settled my spirit. In Hebrews 13:20,21, it states, "May the God of Peace…equip you with everything good for doing His will, and may He work in us what is pleasing to Him, through Jesus Christ, to whom be glory for ever and ever." I was reminded through that scripture that my efforts to follow God's will did not end with the Termination of Parental Rights hearing. I was encouraged that the Lord would "equip" both Joel and I for the exhausting, joyful and all-encompassing task of parenting three children. I sensed God's pleasure. Feeling at peace, I walked the last block home.

When I opened the front door, I was barraged by a crying baby, a hungry husband and two school-age children needing homework help. Yep, it would be a long journey, but one that I would not travel alone.

Scripture

Hebrews 13:20, 21
May the God of Peace…equip you with everything good for doing His will, and may He work in us what is pleasing to Him, through Jesus Christ, to whom be glory for ever and ever.

Thoughts Along the Way

Do you have your poster paper and paint ready?

30

WHIPPED CREAM SPLATTERS

Finalization

In contrast to how slow the adoption process felt prior to Annika's birth, once she was born the days flew by. We marveled at her growth, and I shuffled through the sleepless nights of infancy. Joel was my hero, feeding, diapering and getting Annika down while I napped in the early evening so that I could withstand the middle-of-the night feedings.

Her temperament was easygoing and her spirit light. She was on-the-go, accompanying her two older siblings who raced at full speed in sports and extra-curricular activities. I was amazed with Annika's comfortable acceptance of listening to the Crofton Elementary School's sixth grade band concerts with blaring horns and thumping drums. Snuggled in the baby carrier, she also attended noisy swim meets at the Naval Academy pool in Annapolis. We were learning about her little life as she was learning about ours. It seemed that the bigger the better. "Extroverted" and "tough" were the words we used to describe Annika.

As we settled into daily life, we never lost sight of the fact that Annika's life was such a precious gift, literally given to us by an unselfish and loving couple. Caroline and Michael were often present in our thoughts, and we prayed for their grief and healing.

Annika drew an outpouring of attention—not just from us but also from perfect strangers. Her contagious smile and gorgeous curls were natural magnets. While at a school event for Kelsey and Alex, a reporter from the local paper approached me and commented on her beauty. I smiled and agreed, as any proud parent would. I went on to explain how blessed we felt to have Annika through adoption. After sharing our story, the reporter excitedly asked if she could run a story on our adoption. She expressed that her purpose would be to illuminate the positive process of adoption, especially the largely unknown option of independent adoption. I agreed.

Over the next week, she asked questions, and I provided information. One short week later, I went for an early morning run. As I set out on my normal trek up the tree-lined street, I was distracted by our neighbor's, Ms. Maria, blooming fall garden, causing me to literally trip over our story on the front page of Ms. Maria's newspaper. I stopped, sat down on the chilly sidewalk and stared at our family of five that made the front cover of the paper. I read a beautiful story on adoption. In that article, I learned of a family's calling to adopt, a selfless decision by a birth mother and birth father, and the coming together of two families to ensure the love and care of an unborn child. It was a sweet story. It had taken five years to unfold, but as I read it, I saw in its totality a kaleidoscope of God's constant guidance.

As I folded up the paper and tossed it to Ms. Maria's front door, the Lord spoke one word to me: "Testimony." As a wise friend in our Alabama small group once said, "The only Bible someone may ever have is you." That day, while literally leaping over our story on driveways during my morning run, the Lord put on my heart the importance of testifying to His greatness through our adoption.

The last step in this process had finally arrived; the next day we would finalize Annika's adoption in the state of Maryland. Most states have a post-adoption waiting period in which there are social worker visits and reports to assure the courts that all is well in the family. Over the previous six months, we had completed the required visits, attended all of Annika's doctor's appointments and signed more paperwork.

I thought about the newspaper story. I'm not sure it is possible to accurately communicate just *how* exhausting this long, surprising, unpredictable, joyous, desperate, all-consuming adoption process had been. And now, it was finally over.

The night before Annika's adoption was finalized, I laid down in bed and felt the relief of "all is done"—just as on Christmas eve, when after all the gifts are wrapped, bows are tied, cookies are put out for Santa and the coffee is in the pot set to "auto" to come on at 5:45 a.m.

The next morning I awoke to a quiet house (which was a miracle in and of itself), and as I thought about what to wear and sipped my coffee, the realization of the finality was most comforting. The kids pounded down the stairs, and the race began. Kelsey had to have just the right dress, and Alex thought his tennis shoes needed to match his suit pants. Joel looked striking in a civilian suit (a nice change of pace from camouflage), and Annika was the cutest of all, dressed in a precious hand-made outfit by her grandmother, with shiny patent leather shoes in which to toddle around the courthouse. She held Alex and Kelsey's hands as she practiced walking down the stark white tile hallways of the courthouse.

Entering the courtroom, we met up with our attorney Mark. We waved, and he nodded. With thousands of adoptions under his belt, he was our witness and expert counsel to the judge certifying our adoption as complete on November 15, 2012.

After the Judge struck her gavel declaring Annika ours, we walked out of the colonial style, brick courthouse in the town of Annapolis. That courthouse was just steps from where George Washington addressed the Continental Congress. This historical site punctuated the end of our adoption story.

With a skip in our step, we walked the cobblestone streets until we came to a diner on the quaint main street of Annapolis. Chick and Ruth's Diner is an old favorite of residents and tourists alike. Small, cramped, cash-only and cluttered with historic sailing memorabilia, we could not even fit Annika's stroller through the front door, and so we simply left it on the sidewalk. Joel slid the yellow, vinyl chair out for me as the waitress brought over a high chair for Annika. She looked curiously at us and then, as though a light-bulb had been turned on, exclaimed, "You're the family that adopted! I read about you in the paper." We nodded and smiled, and she sweetly knelt down next to Annika and said, "What a lucky little girl you are to have such a loving family."

The waffles piled high with whipped cream and strawberries arrived, but before eating, we prayed. Holding hands, we closed our eyes and thanked the Lord for his goodness and grace in our lives. In Isaiah 30:18, it states, "Yet the LORD longs to be gracious to you, He rises to show you compassion. For the LORD is a God of justice. Blessed are all who wait for Him!" Our five-year wait was over. As we chuckled at the spatters of whipped cream on all our children's faces, we felt God's blessing in the depths of our souls and in the lightness of our spirits.

Scripture

Isaiah 30:18
Yet the LORD longs to be gracious to you, He rises to show you compassion. For the LORD is a God of justice. Blessed are all who wait for Him!

Thoughts Along the Way

When you get to the day of finalization, give yourself space to celebrate. Do not make extra work for yourself, no huge planning or prep needs to take place, but in simple form celebrate the goodness of the Lord and the love of family in your life. It could be as simple as a whip cream splatter.

31

A STONE OF HOPE

Our Experience with Transracial Adoption

Most households run on a schedule. Our daily routine prior to Annika's arrival changed based on the needs of our children's education, Joel's demanding job and my obligations at the college. All this took second place as we kept pace caring for our sweet baby, Annika. The arrival of an infant added to the business of life, but it also made us slow down to inspect and admire each and every wrinkle on her chubby legs and get swooped into her fits of giggles. Like all new parents, we toughed out sleepless nights spent warming bottles and changing diapers. Yes, I had done all this before, although I was younger then, and I forgot how demanding a baby's needs can be. I persevered through the first year, catching what sleep I could between feedings and carpools. As Joel lulled Annika into dreamland on his chest one evening so I could bank an extra hour of sleep, I thought to myself, "My husband has never looked so sexy."

That first year we lived in a bit of a haze. As the sun rose, I staggered to the kitchen, prepared breakfast and packed lunches. Each morning's crescendo was the dash to the car with Annika bundled up on my hip and the kids piling into the back seat. Typically, on the short drive home from school, Annika's lids got heavy. As I entered the house, the stillness invited a rest. With my baby still asleep in my arms, I dozed off sitting on the couch, but I felt as if I were in heaven.

This was my world, made new by the presence of a newborn baby. There was nothing notably startling about it. Every mother experiences the same tugs and pulls of the insatiable needs of a newborn. Just the same, every mother appreciates how precious these times are!

One such precious moment is seared into my memory. When Annika was just a little over one year of age, she was just toddling, could say "juice" and "mama" and loved her personalized pacifier that said, "My Brother Rocks." Spring was approaching, and we couldn't wait to get outside in the sunshine again. Joel and I decided on a weekend outing to see the newly erected, enormous Martin Luther King Memorial in Washington D.C. We took the Metro into D.C. and made our way to the banks of the Potomac River. With Annika in the stroller, we set out on a walk amidst the deep pink and vibrant purple cherry blossoms.

The winding path along the Potomac eventually led to the towering stone statue of Martin Luther King. We meandered along, people passing us with smiles and an occasional "hello." Then, something struck me: there were no stares, no questions. Our adopted daughter, who was clearly a different race than we are, did not turn heads.

For Joel and I, the race of our adopted child was a non-issue. However, I was somewhat unsure how Annika's biracial identity would be received. Our adoption was devoid of any condemning voices or even quiet whispers of racism. Our family has yet to experience a negative comment or reaction to our biracial beauty. Having said that, I absolutely acknowledge that there are still areas of our country experiencing prejudice. I realized that sad truth after our one-year stint living in Montgomery, Alabama (pre-adoption), where we witnessed deep-seated discrimination. But that morning's D.C. journey proved to be more than just a visit to a tourist attraction. It was confirmation that we live in a country and a society that has, to a large degree, moved beyond discrimination based on the color of one's skin. This reality was only afforded to us because of Martin Luther King and countless others, who bravely worked to clear the cloud of discrimination.

When we arrived at the base of the statue, I literally stood at the feet of Dr. King and looked up at this giant agent of change, and my heart overflowed with thankfulness for his actions and influence. I parked Annika's stroller beneath the quote etched on the side of the monument, which read, "Out of the mountain of despair, a stone of hope." I was moved by the applicability of that statement as it relates to adoption.

Adoption, in most all cases, stems from a situation that amounts to a mountain of despair. Yet, a child's future, secure in the arms of an adoptive family, stands as a stone of hope for both that child, the adoptive family and even the birth mother and birth father.

Dr. King's legacy stands as the hope for our society to overcome racial prejudice and simply live as equals. That afternoon, we unpacked our picnic lunch near a cherry blossom tree. I watched Annika pick up a caterpillar. Alex and Kelsey spread her chubby fingers to allow the creature to crawl from left hand to right hand. They showed her how to gently place the caterpillar in the grass. Martin Luther King gazed down at us and, for an instant, I thought I saw him smile.

Annika has bridged an invisible separation between white and black. With Annika in our arms, we have experienced spontaneous conversations with African-American families. These occur while grocery shopping or in the bleachers while watching Kelsey and Alex at sporting events. I suppose it is natural for people to be drawn to those who have perceived similarities. Just a few short months after our visit to the MLK monument, this was fully illustrated while on vacation at Catalina Island, 26 miles off the California coast.

Joel, with Annika poised on top of his shoulders, and I weaved our way through the mostly Caucasian crowds on the pedestrian walkway. As we passed two African-American women, they stopped and commented on our gorgeous baby. While grabbing her scrumptious thighs, one of the women smiled and exclaimed, "Oh, she reminds me of my grandbaby" and "Look at those amazing curls; they look just like my niece's." As they pulled up pictures on their phone to share, Joel and I with Annika in our lives, felt welcomed and accepted. We also felt more secure initiating friendships with African-American families and had a new appreciation for the nuances of a different ethnicity such as the hours and effort it takes to care for curly hair. Annika opened doors to communities where we once felt we had no place.

Joel and I are invested in issues of race and with added intensity now that we have Annika. It is with the same fervor that we address gender issues for our oldest daughter, Kelsey. I remember Joel becoming much more alert to statements and statistics about glass ceilings and boundaries to athleticism after we had Kelsey. With Annika, we do not want any discrimination to limit her possibilities in life. Thus, the England household pays close attention to political and societal outcries having to do with prejudice and discrimination.

We are thankful that the Lord has not only given us the gift of our biracial beauty but also for leaders in our nation who have helped to eradicate discrimination and prejudice. In a letter from the apostle Paul to the Galatians he says, "There is neither Jew nor Gentile, neither slave nor free, nor is there male and female, for you are all one in Christ Jesus." (Galatians 3:28) We have never felt more as one with our multi-cultural community than we have since welcoming Annika into our family.

Scripture

Galatians 3:28
There is neither Jew nor Gentile, neither slave nor free, nor is there male and female, for you are all one in Christ Jesus.

Thoughts Along the Way

Have you considered race in your adoption?

What concerns exist for you about raising a child in a multi-cultural family?

32

BUILDING A TOWER

Moving Forward as a Parent

I moved to Texas straight out of college. Malibu, California to San Angelo, Texas was a clash of cultures. I was made fun of for my shoes, my lingo (using the word "like" excessively), and the fact that I pronounced Ro-de-o, Ro-da-o (as in Rodeo Drive). They could not get over my California tendencies, and nicknamed me Cali Ali. I could not get over their overuse of the word 'fix.' If you are a Texan and you are going to the grocery store, you would say, "I'm fixin' to go to the grocery store." My co-worker was "fixin" to break up with her boyfriend and my neighbor was "fixin" to buy a new Chevy pick-up. This word slightly irritated me after a while, so when I heard our pastor speak the word "fixed" in church, I had a visceral reaction. Blah, overused. But I was drawn into a story about a woman who had a terminal illness and became "fixed" upon the Lord. The pastor went on to explain her journey and how her eyes were "fixed" on God throughout her struggles. You could not distract her; her head would not budge from her gaze upon the glorious Lord. Although her health outlook was grim, the joy she maintained in life was brighter than the brightest light.

That is how I see you also, "fixed" on the Lord. You have overcome obstacles in your journey that have brought light and truth into your life and those around you.

I am assuming that if you are reading this book in chronological order, then you have arrived at the end-point of your adoption and congratulations are in order! Your relentless pursuit of His will for your life has led you to the final chapter in adoption-your child. You made it!

You have pedaled in the back seat. You have jumped through hoops and stayed still when all you wanted to do was move forward. You may have traveled by air or by land, hiked over mountains of paperwork and navigated turbulent waters of tears to make it where you are right now. Take a breath, friend. You did it. Hold your child in your arms, kiss that sweet forehead and be filled with the peace of the Lord.

This is your picture, the one you longed for six months ago or nine months ago or 2 years ago when you were lost in nowhere Adoptionville. If you had only seen today, this moment, how much confidence would you have had that adoption was a sure-fire bet? How much less stress would you have felt if you had received a "in a year *from* today" Facebook post from the Lord with you and your child cuddled on the couch? The Lord loves the faith you demonstrated these past months and years. You did exactly what is explained in Hebrews 11:1, "Faith is being sure of what we hope for and certain of what we do not see." You could not see His finished work for your family, but you kept on, you did not give in, you believed. And our God is loving on you right now. Stop right now and hear him saying, "Well done, sweet child."

You are probably still in post-adoption hyper-vigilance mode, and now are heading into parenting hyper-vigilance mode. Before you leap from one to the other, there is a key concept from psychology to keep in mind. Humans were not made to withstand long periods of stress. One of the most well known theories regarding stress is Hans Selye's General Adoption Syndrome (GAS is the acronym I use in class). He explains that there are 3 distinct steps that your body goes through when you are stressed; Alarm Stage, Resistance Stage and the Exhaustion Stage. The Alarm Stage is that initial fight or flight response your body has to a stressful situation. The Resistance Stage is when the initial emergency situation has lessened, but you still remain on guard and ready to attend to the situation. Then the last step is the Exhaustion Stage. This is probably where you stand, as your stress has been persistent for a long period of time and your body and immune system is on the verge of shut down. Hear me out-as you step off the adoption train, you need to give yourself space and time to recuperate from this process. I know you are thinking, "But how? I have a baby to feed every three hours?" or "I am a parent now, I can't stop, I just started." For your health and well-being, you need to carve out time for yourself. In order for you to move forward as an attentive and available parent, you must shift gears, and I mean down-shift. To avoid running out of GAS, try writing in a journal, going for a run, or meeting up with a good friend. Process, appreciate and really absorb what has just transpired in your life. Allow the stress to drain from your bones as you cuddle and love on the gift of life the Lord has given you.

I want to share one final piece of scripture from Joshua 4:2-7:

> "Choose twelve men from among the people, one from each tribe, and tell them to take up twelve stones from the middle of the Jordan, from right where the priests are standing, and carry them over with you and put them down at the place where you stay tonight."

> Joshua called together the twelve men he had appointed from the Israelites, one from each tribe, and said to them, "Go over before the ark of the LORD your God into the middle of the Jordan. Each of you is to take up a stone on his shoulder, according to the number of the tribes of the Israelites, to serve as a sign among you. In the future, when your children ask you, 'What do these stones mean?' tell them…"

Let us tell our friends, family and even strangers about God's grace through adoption. Take a hike and choose a rock. Just how the Lord instructed Joshua and his men to take "stones from the middle of the Jordan," I am asking you to find a stone. Paint it. Decorate it. Bedazzle the heck out of it. Put it on display in your home. Finally, post it in the closed Facebook group, Tandem: Adopting with God in the Lead: https://www.facebook.com/groups/adoptiondevotional/.
Let's collectively build a virtual tower of stones that will be seen by all awaiting adoptive parents. That stone will be your talking point for testimony of God's great love for you, your child and also your birth family. He has made beauty from ashes, and you get to tell the gorgeous story, not just to your child but also to all of us!

I can't wait to see your stones, hear your stories, and be inspired by your triumph through hardship. Sisters and brothers in Christ - go, be parents and share your story.

Scripture

Hebrews 11:1
Now faith is confidence in what we hope for and assurance about what we do not see.

Joshua 4:2-7
"Choose twelve men from among the people, one from each tribe, and tell them to take up twelve stones from the middle of

the Jordan, from right where the priests are standing, and carry them over with you and put them down at the place where you stay tonight."

So Joshua called together the twelve men he had appointed from the Israelites, one from each tribe, and said to them, "Go over before the ark of the LORD your God into the middle of the Jordan. Each of you is to take up a stone on his shoulder, according to the number of the tribes of the Israelites, to serve as a sign among you. In the future, when your children ask you, 'What do these stones mean?' tell them that the flow of the Jordan was cut off before the ark of the covenant of the LORD. When it crossed the Jordan, the waters of the Jordan were cut off. These stones are to be a memorial to the people of Israel forever.

Thoughts Along the Way

Go to the Facebook group, Tandem: Adopting with God in the Lead and post your stone. (This is a closed group, so you will just request join the group and state that you are reading *Tandem*. Although closed groups are visible in a Facebook search, the content posted on this group's Timeline is visible on a members-only basis.)

NOTES

Chapter 1 - An Old Country Road: The Beginning

1. Warren, R. (2002). *The purpose driven life*. Grand Rapids, MI: Zondervan.

Chapter 7 - Johnnie Walker Red Moments: Ruling Out Options and Zeroing In

1. Child Welfare Information Gateway (2016). *Trends in US adoptions: 2008-2012*. Retrieved from www.childwelfare.gov/pubPDFs/adopted0812.pdf

Chapter 9 - Your New Part-Time Job: Carving Out Time for Adoption

1. Shakespeare, W., Mowat, B. A., & Werstine, P. (2012). *The tragedy of Hamlet, Prince of Denmark*. New York: Simon & Schuster Paperbacks.

Chapter 11 - More than a Basket of Fruit: Health, Finances and Support

1. Gumm, J. (2014). *You can adopt without debt*. Nashville, TN: The United Methodist Publishing House.

Chapter 14 - The Places You Will Go: Choosing a Birth Mom in Accordance with God's Will

1. Seuss, D. (1990). *Oh the places you'll go!* New York: Random House.

2. Moore, B. (2016). *Entrusted: A study of 2 Timothy*. Nashville, TN: LifeWay Press.

3. Soanes, C. & Stevenson, A. (2009). *Oxford dictionary of English*. Oxford: Oxford University Press.

Chapter 19 - Canyon: Empathizing with Your Birth Mom

1. Rogers, C. (1980). *A way of being*. New York, NY: Houghton Mifflin Company.

2. Cushman, L. F., Kalmuss, D., & Namerow, P. B. (1993). Placing an infant for adoption: The experiences of young birthmothers. *Social Work*, *38*(3), 264-272. doi: 10.1093/sw/38.3.264

Chapter 22 - Hit The Floor: When an Expectant Mother Changes Her Mind

1. *The adoption book: Successful private adoption.* (2016) Washington D.C.: Families for Private Adoption.

2. Thatcher, S. (2015). *Saying goodbye to "our" twins.* Retrieved from https://inourlittleredhouse.com/2015/10/

Chapter 23 - Erikson and Identity: Our Choice for an Open Adoption

1. Siegel, D. H., & Smith, S. L. (2012). *Openness in adoption: From secrecy and stigma to knowledge and connections.* New York, NY: Evan B. Donaldson Adoption Institute.

2. Brodzinsky, D. (2006). Family structural openness and communication openness as predictors in the adjustment of adopted children. *Adoption Quarterly*, 9, 1-18. doi:10.1300/J145v09n04_01

3. Farr, R. H., Grant-Marsney, H. A., & Grotevant, H. D. (2014). Adoptees' contact with birth parents in emerging adulthood: The role of adoption communication and attachment to adoptive parents. *Family Process, 53* (4), 656-671. doi:10.1111/famp.12069

Chapter 24 - Dial Tone: Normalizing Doubt

1. Moore, B. (2008). *Esther: It's tough being a woman.* Nashville, TN: LifeWay Press.

Chapter 26 - In the Birthing Room: Impossibility of Reciprocity

1. Stott, J. (2012). *Basic Christianity.* Downers Grove, IL, Inter-Varsity Press.

Chapter 27 - 23 Steps Away: Choosing Love

1. Birthmothers who change their minds about adoption. (n.d.). *Family Education.* Retrieved from http://life.familyeducation.com/adoption/birth-parents/45794.html?page=1

ACKNOWLEDGMENTS

This book was truly a team effort. I am eternally grateful for the support I received in getting this devotional to print!

Dad, you are my ultimate encourager. Your expert guidance enabled my thoughts that were once scratched on the backsides of receipts and church bulletins to become a published book. I have witnessed your faith grow deeper and your understanding of God's amazing ways gain clarity through our teamwork on this book.

Mom, you are my rock. You have demonstrated Christ's love on earth through your unconditional love for me. By example, you have taught me how to be a strong woman, one that can have a career and also be a dedicated mother. Thank you for allowing me to be the keeper of the smelly-sticker drawer at your classroom desk. In little ways and big ones you have made me feel special all my life.

My husband, Joel, our marriage stands as my most prized accomplishment in life. From that softball field in D.C. to the desert of Arizona, we have trekked a lot of territory. We are *good*-so good together. I am amazed how you can be so committed to all your worlds. You seamlessly weave together our family, your career, and our marriage; making time for even the smallest of details like playing Booshka-Wooshkas on the floor with our kids, or sending me flowers for no particular occasion. Thank you for allowing me to carve out time for this book.

My children, Kelsey, Alex, and Annika-my most blessed moments in life are with you. When you cuddle with me at night, give me a hug that cures the woes of a bad day, when we read books together and laugh, or when I stare at you in your sleep, I am overwhelmed with pride for the faithful persons you are becoming. I am joyful beyond belief with you in my life. Thank you for making your own turkey-sandwiches for lunch while I wrote this devotional!

Phil and Donna England, I appreciate your willingness to jump on planes to help us out! Your love overflows for our children-that is a priceless gift.

I want to thank my incredible team of editors; Edward Jones, Elizabeth Lyons, Karen Shively, Wolf and Jami Jones, Joel England, Ann Jones, Sarah Thatcher, and Katherine Infantino.

Our dear birth family, Caroline, Michael and Julia, your gift to us was life and your continued gift to Annika is your love. Thank you for your unselfish and unconditional love. There are no words to adequately express our gratitude.

ABOUT THE AUTHOR

Alison England is a Christian, adoptive mother. The combination of her faith and career experience in social work, prompted her to write *Tandem.* She has been married for over 20 years to her husband, Joel. Together they have three children, the youngest is adopted.

She cofounded Momentum Adoptions, a licensed adoption agency and is a professor at Arizona State University. Alison's passion to encourage adoptive parents extends through the TandemAdoption.com ministry, including her Christian adoption blog and speaking engagements. She also volunteers as the President of the West-Coast Chapter of Families for Private Adoption non-profit.

For the past 21 years, the England family has traveled the United States, as her husband was active duty military. They are now settled in the sunny state of Arizona.

For more information on Alison's adoption ministry or to schedule her for a speaking engagement, go to:
www.tandemadoption.com

You can also join the Tandem: Adopting with God in the Lead closed group on Facebook to gain encouragement and support on your adoption journey.

Made in the USA
Middletown, DE
22 May 2020